Real Man

Real Dad

Real Talk

Real Nigga

Real Man
Real Dad
Real Talk
Real Nigga

Gary B. Clifton

Published by:

Gassaway, ALG
bgassaway1@gmail.com

092319602020

First Edition © 2020 by Gary B. Clifton

Dedication

This book is dedicated to my wife, family, and Curtis Purnell "Born" Williams a mighty street soldier who turned his life around and was on his way to doing some amazing things before meeting an untimely death as a result of gun violence. RIP my brother!

Foreward

Real Man, Real Dad, Real Talk, and Real Nigga is Gary Clifton's mosaic. Gary weaves together pieces of his life to create a beautiful story. If someone asked me to describe Gary with one word, it would be *love*. In this epic tale, Gary shares his love for family, friends, fathers, youths, community, and Black people in general.

Whether you were born in the '60s, '70s, '80s, or '90s, Gary's life is a true reflection of your life. While you might not have had the same experiences, you can definitely make clear connections between his experiences and your own.

Gary did an extraordinary job laying out his values of honesty, loyalty, fairness, integrity, tenacity, family, friendship, brotherhood, and fatherhood.

After reading this book, I am clear why I made the following declaration: "If I were in a foxhole during the most heated battle, I would want to be in it with Gary." I believe with all my being that Gary would fight to the end to watch my back, as I would watch his back, even at the ultimate cost of our lives. That is Gary Clifton.

As a former New York City superintendent, principal, and teacher, I strongly endorse this book for all high school students (even mature middle school students). However, I doubt school administrators will allow students to read it in schools because of a few "profane" words that Gary thought significant enough not to remove to appease anyone. That speaks directly to Gary's character. The lesson for me is sometimes the smallest things are the most significant.

As a community, we should be obligated to get this book into our neighbors' households, community libraries, community centers, colleges and universities, and even our public schools.

Gary is an urban griot. He tells stories that embody what most of us, living in the hood, can connect with palpably. He writes of the past, present, and future. He is prophetic in many ways.

There is universality to Gary's story. While I know we are the same age, we were raised in different hoods; yet, our lives share so many parallels. I am certain as you read the book, you too, regardless of your age, will likewise find stunning similarities.

Gary epitomizes fatherhood—not Black fatherhood, but fatherhood period. As I read his tales and guidance to Black fathers, I could feel the emotions he must have felt as he was writing. His love for them and their promise is profound.

Gary gives great guidance to our children. He reflects on his own childhood. His story about his egg and cheese ritual is metaphorical and still practiced by children in the hood.

Throughout the book, Gary goes to great lengths to speak to the importance of family and the roles that parents can and should play. He clearly believes that parenting is a major component of the social, political, and economic success of the Black community. Children will repeat what they experience. Gary points out how important it is for him to practice what he preaches. This is what he wants all adults to do, particularly because of their profound influence on children.

I am so happy that Gary is sharing his life stories, which are full of wisdom, guidance, and prophecy. The world will now know what many of those close to Gary have known for some time: Gary is a gift. Gary is a griot. Gary is a living Black legend.

Bernard Gassaway, Ed.D.

Table of Contents

Part One

Shoeshine Boy - My first job (hustle) was as a shoeshine boy at nine years old. I took the Q6 to Sutphin Boulevard and Jamaica Avenue and walked to the courthouse, where I noticed right away that the Whites wore suits, and most of the Blacks wore everyday clothes. It was 1969, and most of the people on the bus were women. It is funny to me now, but things haven't changed all that much. Very few of the Blacks had their shoes shined at this time. My greatest memory was after working for a couple of hours, I had enough to go to "Big Daddies" and get french fries, frank, and soda and still have change left. I was very short my whole life, so until I was eleven, I never had to pay to ride the bus. This enabled me to see so much at a young age. Jamaica Avenue, at this time, was the biggest area that I had ever seen with its stores, movie theaters, people, and the tall buildings all around.

My brother and I were responsible children, and it was nothing for us to journey there regularly. Today, there are not a lot of responsible children because parents are not effective teachers. Parents are afraid of their children. My mother loved us, but she didn't take shit from us, and we knew that. In most ways, she set a great example, including keeping a spotless home, always being on time, making sure we had food, and disciplining us when necessary. While we took public transportation when we were not traveling with relatives or one of my mother's connections, we always had great clothes and plenty of food. She also took us places regularly. As young children, my brother and I would fly alone to meet relatives in Florida and Georgia. My mother and aunt would always take us out to eat, so after a while, it became normal for us to go to the pizza shop, a local diner, or for us to earn some money and then go to a burger joint and sit down and eat. As young boys, my brother and I could be found in a diner like old truckers. While in some ways, I seemed to be mature, in other ways, I picked up bad habits, including cursing like a sailor and being a crybaby when I didn't get my way. Later, these things would get me in trouble, but overall, between school,

1

sports, and hustling for a dollar, I managed to stay clear of major trouble.

During my early years and throughout my life, my brother and I never missed having a father. In fact, we weren't the only ones on the block who didn't have one, so we were never isolated. At this time, my brother became my primary protector, and although I would have many more, he remains that today. We never had a babysitter in our lives. Today, I believe they call that a latchkey child. That is bullshit. You are a responsible person at a young age. If you are taught to be responsible, you will be. Even though we had three daughters, my wife and I would employ our own version of this system years later with much success. Today, almost every child has a cell phone, and many are doing the dumbest shit, so go figure.

My brother and I were issued keys and told don't lose them or else. I can remember looking all over the schoolyard a couple of times until I found my key. When my brother and I would get home from school, we would call my mother at work to check in. I can still remember the number today, FA2-9399. We didn't need area codes in the '60s. After that, we would do our homework, then put on our play clothes, and then go outside to play. Yes, we had play clothes back then, and, in some cases, it made a difference. School was treated differently, and there was a difference in what you wore each day. My brother and I were very well dressed and had handkerchiefs with our initials on them. We took great care of our clothes, a good habit I still practice. My mother had several rules for her children, including what happens in the house stays in the house; a rule that many would question today with child abuse being a major issue. You can eat whatever you want; just clean the kitchen. Never use the stove or oven. Go to school. Mind your business. If someone hits you, you better hit him back, and most of all, never fight each other. We never did!

Mrs. Deale – *"From Nine to Three, you belong to me. Let me be proud of you."*

The saying above was clearly posted on the board as soon as you entered our classroom. Mrs. Deale was both my fifth and sixth-grade teacher. She was very strict but very approachable and, at times, could be very sweet and showed us affection. Our classes were the top class each year, and everyone in the class had excellent reading and math scores. We also had the same room with the same seats. We were a special group of students coming from very different family make-ups, and Mrs. Deale understood that. Being unprepared was a big mistake, but not having your homework was a crime. Mrs. Deale did not hesitate to embarrass you to the point that you would almost cry, and to be honest, a couple of times, I did. I was not the only one, and students would pretend to be sick and stay home if they did not complete their homework. Mrs. Deale would check your homework personally, and when she assigned monitors, you had better tell the truth. Mrs. Deale was a real teacher who understood that students needed to be responsible. Mrs. Deale had the best penmanship that I have ever seen and was compulsively neat. Anyone who knows me knows that I am compulsively neat but can't write for shit. One day, I handed in a sloppy assignment. Mrs. Deale tore it up in front of the whole class and told me to do it over and bring it in the next day. I was shocked, and at lunch, I went into the bathroom and sobbed for a minute. I pulled myself together and, after school, rushed home and redid the assignment putting the right effort into it. The next day, when it was my turn to be graded, she observed it and gave me an A+. She put it on the bulletin board and told the class what an excellent job I had done. This was a teaching moment for Mrs. Deale, and she understood this better than any teacher I have ever met. Later that day, she hugged me and said there will be times when you will not get a second chance, so make the most of the first opportunity. After that, I never did a half-ass job again on any assignment throughout my schooling.

One of our great class competitions was the loose-leaf competition, where Mrs. Deale would check everyone's binder to ensure that everything was in order, I never won, and usually, the winners were the girls, Terri Abney, Diane Dillahunt, Robin Dixon, or Sandra Barnes. I can tell you everyone had their shit in order, and when we did, she rewarded us with a party. We had more parties than anyone in school history, but we learned so much. The next year, we went to middle school, and we were all in the top classes. One of my fondest memories was we performed the play *A Christmas Carol* by Charles Dickens. I would later read *Tale of Two Cities* by Dickens because Mrs. Deale introduced us to positive reading, and that stayed with us for our entire lives. The play was totally engrossed in White culture, but that was the era we were living in. I had a very small role of Tiny Tim with one line, "God bless us all, everyone," but I said it like I was the primary character of the play and got a standing ovation. There was no jealousy from any of us regarding roles. We just wanted to put on the best play possible for Mrs. Deale, and we did.

I never met anyone like Mrs. Deale after sixth grade; in fact, some of us started our street lives after this period. One of my best friends, David Williams, was in Mrs. Deale's class together with me and often shared stories about Mrs. Deale. Years later, Dave and I both spent a lot of time in the street and saw each other in some tough situations. However, I was a little luckier. Dave is a perfect example of a genius who was pulled into the streets. Dave died a couple of years ago after some tough times. He had turned his life around, and I was so proud of him. When I saw Dave, I was always happy because he was someone I knew I could count on no matter what the situation was, and I mean no matter what it was. Dave did a great job of raising his son and growing as a man. Mrs. Deale has stayed with us forever, and we both admitted later that thinking of Mrs. Deale at times stopped us from going too far in some bad situations. Other teachers could not scare us or intimidate us. We knew they didn't really care, and after that, neither did we. While I was always a very good student, I never really had any other teachers who had an impact on my life. Teaching is a special job, and too many people get into teaching for the wrong reasons. We continue to blame children while a significant percentage of the teachers are not qualified to teach. Just because someone has completed the academic component, we throw them in a classroom and expect them to teach our children. To be a teacher, you should love children, and if not, please find another occupation. Love is patient, understanding, tough, and strong. It brings both joy and sorrow and will add and subtract from your life, so understand this before you walk into the classroom.

In some cases, some of the students have more common sense than the teachers and figure out quickly they are being short-changed. I have spent time in many schools since then, running programs and working with teachers and administrators and have posed the question of students remaining with teachers for more than one year like we did with Mrs. Deale, and to date, no one has ever really given me an answer. Today, we see new models for schools where the building is sectioned off into several schools. Whose idea was this? We also have the public versus charter argument. Now, we even have metal detectors. The bottom line is, we have too many people involved in education who have no idea what they are doing. In addition, a lot of money is being distributed to consultants, teachers, administration, and security, but children are still not learning. Unions are involved whose primary goal is to get top benefits and pay for their members at the expense of our children. Poor communities usually have poor-performing schools with teachers and administrators who are not willing to go the extra mile for the children. Many of these people send their kids to better schools where they live and have no desire to have their children spend any time around the children they teach. On the way back to where they live, many of them talk about us as if they have left the zoo and share these stories with their friends. Many of them are so arrogant that they really believe they are doing us a favor by showing up in our communities as if their presence is needed. Moving forward, we need to get rid of many of the people involved in education today to fix the problem. If that means our communities suffer for that period, so be it. If not, the cycle of rubber rooms, poor reading and math scores, sexual encounters of teachers and students, and flat out miseducation will continue. Yes, miseducation is alive and well in many areas of the United States with no cure in sight. People currently in power do not want us to get our shit together. They use the educational system to ensure that they stay in control. I will challenge anyone on that.

Let me be clear. Parents also play a major role in the failure of the educational system, with many of them showing little interest in their children. We know that these schools are not set up for success, yet many of us do not put in the necessary work to ensure our children receive the proper education. We make excuses for not attending PTA meetings and other important educational sessions but will be the first at the talent show. Many of the parents are fucked up people; I do not know a better way to say it. How else can you explain selling out your child? I have witnessed this on many occasions with my own eyes. I am not an advocate for prisons, but I wish there was another way to punish some of you for not ensuring that your child is properly educated. Black men, you must take a stronger stand when it comes to education. I know they don't want us in the schools, but you must find a way to overcome that obstacle. Whether you live with your children or not, it is your duty to get and stay involved in the education of your children. Sad but true, when I enter a school, I treat it as a prison or a court. I empty my pockets and have identification readily available when necessary. I cooperate to the fullest with school staff because my intent usually involves assisting children. I fully understand that they view me as the enemy as a Black man when I attempt to enter a school, but if I complete my mission, then my child or children win, and that is the primary goal!

168th Street – 144-15 168th Street, Jamaica, NY, 11434 is where we lived for almost twelve years. We had a two-bedroom apartment in a two-family house, which was perfect for my mother, brother, and me. The apartment had new expensive furniture and was always kept clean. The block was predominately Black with two White families who got along with everyone else. The houses were well kept, and there was a "block association" that we never belonged to. My mother was always private and never really wanted to mix with anyone. I understood years later, because she was single and attractive, the other women on the block and the neighborhood were always on alert. It was always funny that all of the men waited to do their chores when they knew she would be returning from work. They would be watering their lawns and working on their cars just smiling and acting all silly when she would walk down the block. My mother would smile and just keep walking. My brother and I never paid for the ice cream man when one of these men was around. We would pocket that money and go to the store and get extra snacks.

My brother and I are both light-skinned with green eyes, so we knew at an early age that we had to be tough because people would try us. Well, the first thing we did was establish that if you got into a fight with one of us, you had to fight us both, and after that, we never really had a problem. Years later, we would become good basketball players, so everything worked out. In our neighborhood, we played baseball, football, and basketball. We formed our own teams, bought uniforms, and gave out awards. As a young boy, I was an organizer and would be out at 6:00 am, waiting for everyone to come out to participate. I was tough on the younger guys on my block, and they respected me and worked hard to be good at whatever sport we played. Now, our block had many family make-ups from two parents to a single parent (mother) to grandparents raising their grandkids. As much as these homes seemed to be so-called respectable, they were functionally dysfunctional at best. There were regular cases of domestic violence, alcoholism, drug addiction, adultery, and crime. Most people played the illegal numbers every day and purchased hot (stolen) property with little hesitation. Many thought that since they were able to purchase a home that they had climbed the social ladder, only to find out later that things had not changed much at all. As I became more involved in the streets in my late teens, I would see some of the adults I admired in a different light. This changed how I viewed people for the rest of my life. I have never judged anyone and will not start now, but I can honestly say that as a minor that I sold drugs to and got high with adults who I respected as a young kid. I will not preach to anyone, but I would like to emphasize to adults, please do not get high with children no matter how mature you think they are. One thing you learn quickly is that drugs make everybody equal. I can remember going to collect money from a well-respected adult in my hood while he was having dinner with his family. He did a good job of keeping it from his wife, but I know that was not a great family moment. At the time, I really didn't think much of it, but later on, I understood how drugs can affect an entire community. Don't get me wrong. I wanted my money, but I became more aware of when to collect.

There were some special people on my block, in particular, Mr. J. He was a lawyer who years later would go on to be a well-respected judge. Mr. J. had one son but would spend time with us playing sports and allowing us to shoot pool in his basement. He would take us to the store and buy us snacks and make sure our bikes were working. My brother and I always speak well about Mr. J. He was always an inspiration to us. He also let us borrow his lawnmower to cut lawns. We started our own businesses, and he saw us trying to do something positive and assisted us. We broke the lawnmower, and you know, he bought a new one and still let us borrow it.

Many of the families living in Queens migrated from other parts of New York City in the '50s, '60s, and '70s. There was a mixture of Brooklyn, the Bronx, Harlem, and then the people originally from Queens, so we were many styles and influences coming together. The Blakes were very special to me. They were a family from the Bronx who taught me a lot about music and family bonding. I spent a lot of time with Barry and Mike in their house, which was always open to my brother and me. Their mother, Ms. Juanita, was always so nice to me. Barry went on to be successful in the financial world, and Mike is a well-respected inspector in the NYC police department. The Benjamins were also from the Bronx, and I spent a lot of time in their house as well. They would listen to the Knicks on the radio, which was so new to me. Momma Benjamin would make pastrami sandwiches, which I loved, and after tasting them, I gave up ham and never went back. The Harrisons were from Harlem, and they also left a positive impression on my life. Karrem (Reggie) and Jaysen were very close to my brother and me, and the two-hand touch football games in the street were legendary. The Harrisons, Strahns, Blakes, Benjamins, Risbrooks, Weathers, Williamses, Joys, Webbs, Joneses, Fergusons, Faulkners, Worthours, Andersons, Harrises, and some I cannot remember, were some great people. We spent some great times together, and I often reminisce about my early childhood. 168th Street was a special block to me, and a part of me sometimes wishes that I would have stayed on the block, but the streets won me over.

After-School and Night Center – It is no coincidence that I have spent a large portion of my adult life in schools, after the regular day session had ended, leading afterschool programs. Some of my fondest memories as a child were spent in both afterschool and night center programs. In my hood, there was P.S. 52 and J.H.S. 231. P.S. 52 was run by Mr. Miller, a no-nonsense gym teacher whose regular job was at J.H.S. 231. Mr. Miller ran both basketball and football tournaments and constantly gave us advice on life. Mr. Miller was White, tall, and had a muscular build. Mr. Miller always appeared to be happy and rarely had any trouble getting everyone to cooperate. I saw some of the toughest guys in the hood give Mr. Miller the utmost respect, and Mr. Miller always made them feel good about who they were. Mr. Miller also introduced us to "dodge ball," a game that could get you a lot of respect in the neighborhood. The game focused on your ability to survive being hit by the ball, and it included people of all ages. Some of the toughest guys in the hood played, and they all wanted to be the last man standing. The rules of the game were you had four seconds to throw the ball as everyone counted one, two, three, four, and try to hit somebody. If you are hit, you are eliminated. If the person catches the ball, then the person who threw it is eliminated. The ball is constantly in motion, and anyone can have access at any time. One session, we started with forty players, and I was one of the final two players left. I was going head to head against Moon Jackson. Moon was one of the toughest motherfuckers I have ever met in my life. He came from the Jackson family, arguably the toughest family in my hood. I witnessed Moon beat a guy so bad that his family moved the next week. Moon chased me around for a while and could not hit me. Finally, I got the ball and cornered Moon and threw the ball as hard as I could only to be heartbroken to see Moon catch it to eliminate me. After that day, Moon went out of his way to always make sure I was all right. This mattered a lot to me because Moon was older and very well respected. No matter what anyone tells you, everybody in the hood needs somebody to look after him or her. This is what is missing today.

Mr. Ross ran the J.H.S. 231 Night Center, and like Mr. Miller, he didn't take shit from anybody. Mr. Ross was Black and very laid back. He spent a lot of time talking with all the kids. I had a great relationship with Mr. Ross. He gave me tips on my game and even came to see me play at other places. I was very short, but still one of the better players and Mr. Ross loved how hard I played. Mr. Ross played surrogate father to so many of us. Years later, I would find myself being Mr. Ross and fully understood why he devoted so much time to us. One night, I remember the police came into the center looking for one of the kids, and Mr. Ross had the kid hide until they left. Immediately after they left, Mr. Ross blasted the kid. He called the kid's mother and told her what had happened and advised her on what to do. Mr. Ross knew that if those police officers would have arrested that kid that anything could happen, including signing a confession for something he didn't do and possibly even something worse. Mr. Ross also wanted all of us to know that the center was someplace we could go for assistance, and if the police came in and started arresting us, then we had nothing, and he didn't want us to ever be hopeless.

I adopted this philosophy in my night programs later in my life. We had all types of so-called killers working out regularly each night. What these guys did outside of the center, we could not control, but inside the building, they were on their best behavior. Guns were well hidden when participants brought them in, and sometimes, we even confiscated them and returned them later with a brief lecture. Cooler heads always prevailed, and most times, we got the beefing parties together and squashed the situation. Drugs were never to be seen, and everyone knew the rules. Disrespect of children and women would not be tolerated, and there was a zero-tolerance level that was strictly enforced. I can remember an incident where we had a newcomer who thought he would do as he pleased. To his surprise, our guys quickly removed him from the building with a very thorough ass whipping, and he never came our way again.

I strongly believe that both afterschool programs and night centers are just as important as what is taught each day. I have operated both afterschool and night center programs for thirty-five years and believe I have impacted thousands of lives. I have no secret formula for success; all I can say is that I am not full of shit like a lot of people that our children encounter each day. I believe that if our children are given guidance, direction, love, and, most of all, understanding, they can be successful. I can't tell you how many times I have worked with youths who have been categorized as problematic (special education) only to find out that they were intelligent, misguided souls in need of direction. I believe that more funding should be given to afterschool and evening programs instead of police, courts, and prisons. We hear calls today to defund the police and place those monies into community programs, I totally agree with that position. If we had centers operating twenty-four hours a day with a staff that included several paid community residents with street credibility, we would have safer communities. Prisons operate twenty-four hours a day, but schools close. Can someone tell me why?

Shaft, Superfly & the Mack – In the early '70s, many of us were thrilled with the start of Black exploitation films. Three of the most popular of the era were *Shaft* starring Richard Roundtree, *Superfly* starring Ron O'Neal, and *The Mack* starring Max Julien and Richard Pryor. There were many others, and Black women were also represented with *Coffey* starring Pam Grier and *Cleopatra Jones* starring Tamara Dobson. These films contained graphic sexual scenes, an abundance of violence, and adult language. These films also displayed many of the characters that we saw each day in the hood, which made them very real to us. Also, these movies were usually shot in urban locations that looked like our neighborhoods. Every week, we would find ourselves in the local theater watching these movies over and over. My mother never worried about movie ratings, and neither did I as a parent. With the exception of X-rated movies, my brother and I saw them all, and so did my children. Besides, you could always find an adult to get you in when needed. Movies were different back in the day. Once you paid your fare, you could watch over and over until you decided to leave. Some weekends, we would spend our entire Saturday at the movies.

This was also a time when many of us started to look at ourselves differently. Before this time, everyone I admired on television and in the movies was White. Now, the main characters in these movies who were winning the fights, getting the money, and ending up with the beautiful woman (a Black woman) looked like me, and it was very exciting. It did not matter to us that Superfly was a drug dealer and the Mack was a pimp; they were beating the White man at the end. In our very short lives, this was the first time that we saw this happen. When we left the theater, my brother and I were ecstatic. We couldn't wait to get home and tell everyone. The closest we ever came to seeing a cool Black man in a role like this was Bill Cosby in *I Spy*, but that was nothing like this. These movies had curses, sex, and violence, and to be honest, I couldn't get enough. We also loved the clothes of the characters, particularly Shaft, Superfly, and of course, the Mack and his full-length white fur coat. I remember we all showed up at a party in plaid pants marshmallow shoes, and full-length maxi coats. You could not tell us that we were not fly or superfly. *Gordon Parks Sr., who had success with an earlier film, The Learning Tree, directed shaft.* Gordon was a modern-day Renaissance man and was a highly successful photographer. His son, Gordon Parks Jr., directed *Superfly*. Both films were made on shoestring budgets but went on to earn millions. Gordon Parks Jr. died at an early age in a plane crash, so we never had the opportunity to see him excel at his craft.

In the '70s, you would never be educated about the talented father and son duo and their great accomplishments. Other actors would follow, including Fred Williamson as *Black Caesar* and Jim Brown as *Slaughter*, both ex-football greats. Three of my favorite films of all time were highlighted by great female performances, including Diane Carroll in *Claudine*, Lonnette McKee, and Irene Cara in *Sparkle* and my favorite, Diana Ross in *Lady Sings the Blues*. Diana Ross's performance in *Lady Sings the Blues* was an Oscar-winning performance, but the haters would never let that happen, especially in the '70s. Berry Gordy, the music genius, did his thing with "Lady" and introduced many of us to Richard Pryor as "Piano Man," another Oscar-winning performance. The other great accomplishment of these movies is that we wrote, directed, and acted. These movies employed us, but our so-called leaders fell to the pressure of the myth of blaxploitation. All we hear now is how hard it is for Blacks and Hispanics to find work in the entertainment industry.

The other major accomplishments of this era were the outstanding movie soundtracks (scores) that were part of these films. These included *Shaft* (Oscar winner) by Isaac Hayes, *Superfly* by Curtis Mayfield, which is the best soundtrack for any movie by far in any era, *The Mack* by Willie Hutch, Claudine performed by Gladys's Knight and written by Curtis Mayfield, *Sparkle* performed by Aretha Franklin and written by Curtis Mayfield, and *Lady Sings the Blues* performed by Diana Ross with the original music of Billie Holiday. *Lady Sings the Blues* was produced by Berry Gordy of Motown and introduced many young people like me to Billie Holiday. It also gave the women, including my mother, Billy D. Williams, the ultimate Black male sex symbol of his era.

These movies have received mixed reviews over the years, including some saying that they were offensive to our heritage. These comments usually come from some house niggas who really didn't understand how these movies raised our self-esteem level, even with some negativity. It was okay for us to watch White Americans as cowboys slaughtering Indians or White soldiers killing other ethnic groups. I can tell you firsthand that when we got back to school on Monday, all we talked about were these movies, and you could see the excitement in our eyes. Remember, each week, all we did was listen and study European and White American history. The only time we talked about ourselves was as slaves, and many of us were tired of that shit. We were intelligent enough to understand that some of the characters were pimps and drug dealers, but these people existed in our communities and, in some cases, treated us with more respect than the teachers and other staff. Most of the teachers that we encountered along the way really didn't understand that we were a proud people who had accomplished a great deal in history. Instead, they went on and on about the accomplishments of White people. Even today, people who are in charge of education continue to make the same mistakes. We have to design the curriculum to include the accomplishments of people of all colors and not be relegated to those they consider safe and will keep them in charge. You wonder why many kids gravitate to the negative elements of the streets? Because the lessons that are being taught highlight White Americans' accomplishments. Imagine if the curriculum in schools included Malcolm, Dubois, Wright, Robeson, Baldwin, and some of the other great minds.

Today, Hollywood is shaking up because of all of the Black content available through HBO, Showtime, Starz, Netflix, Hulu, Amazon, Apple TV, and so many more. Earlier shows like the *Wire*, *Oz*, and some others paved the way for some of the fabulous shows we see today. I love *Power*, directed by 50 Cent and Courtney Kemp, *The Chi* directed by Lena Waite, *Insecure* directed by Issa Rae, *Atlanta*, directed by Donald Glover, just to name a few. I love the fact that Black women are in positions of power in the industry. Gabrielle Union, LaLa Anthony, Megan Goode, Viola Davis, Octavia Spencer are some of my favorites. Tyler Perry is amazing, and the fact that he opened his own studio is so exciting. Over the years, he has employed so many people of color. We were held back for so long. Just think of how many minds could have been positively impacted if we were given the opportunity to create our own content so much sooner?

Farmers Blvd & New York Blvd. (Guy R. Brewer). (Across the Bridge) – I grew up in a hood that always had something going on. We were right next to Kennedy Airport, and when you live by the airport, nothing stops. It was a blue-collar community that was surrounded by factories and other forms of commerce. Many Whites traveled into our community for work each day and owned delicatessens, automotive supply stores, and taverns. This section of Jamaica/Springfield Gardens, Queens, covered from Rockaway Blvd. to Springfield Blvd. across the Belt Parkway. We were unique in that we had access to the world because of the proximity of the airport. We fed off of the traffic of the airport, including the theft and sale of merchandise fresh off the planes, both domestic and international. There was a time when we had the United States Olympic warm-ups and were wearing them in the hood before they could be delivered to Lake Placid for the Winter Games. The drug market was extremely lucrative because we had the clientele of the airport, including pilots, stewardesses, travelers, airport personnel, and, most of all, the truckers and warehouse workers. Many of the Whites would cop from us while they were at work and then return to their communities where no one would have a clue. Some of our best customers were well-respected business people, male and female. Other markets included gambling and prostitution. We had spots all over, including our own cabstand where you could get just about anything you wanted, and I was connected to them all. I really started running the streets when I was about thirteen years old. One of my first hustles was going to the store for the hustlers and the truckers. Two things were important; you had to be fast and had to know how to count. I was very fast and counting money was no problem for me. Soon, my errands turned into making drops for people and eventually getting involved in the illegal numbers racket where the real money was being made. People forget that the illegal numbers racket was a big industry employing a lot of people in the Black community. I have seen some very crafty and elaborate operations in my time. My mother's husband (not my father) was Scotty, who was one of the biggest number bankers in Queens. Scotty was the man with his beautiful house, fancy clothes, and, most of all, his custom

Cadillacs, which were some of the best cars I ever saw, even until today. My mother lived with Scotty, and my brother and I lived in the family apartment around the corner with her making an occasional visit here and there. Let me be clear. We were never poor. We had plenty of food, beautiful expensive clothes, and a nice apartment. We grew up fast but were very respectful teens. Scotty was always nice to me but could also be very stern when he thought it was necessary. Scotty's youngest son Little Scotty was an academic genius, and I consider him my little brother. His life at a young age was very limited because of his father's life style. While he had everything he needed and wanted, he could not play in the neighborhood like other children. It is amazing to see him today as a very mature and wise man co-parenting his daughter. Love you baby bro; you turned out great. While many thought I had it easy working with Scotty, it was the exact opposite; he worked me harder than others.

The money was great, especially for a teen, and I did this until the late '70s when the racket started to fade away when legal numbers came into existence. During my senior year of high school, I lived by myself in the apartment because my brother went to college in California on a basketball scholarship. I was really happy for him. Up to this point, he had navigated the streets without getting involved in some of the things I was doing. Don't get me wrong. He was doing his own thing, but he was cleaner than I was.

When I was about thirteen, I also got my first real legal job at the local stationery/bodega store, Colson's Stationery (Ron's). Before there were bodegas, many stores served as stationery stores, which provided school supplies, batteries, newspapers, personal care items, and groceries. At Ron's, we sold it all. This job would introduce me to a whole new group of people in the hood. These groups of people were just like the hustlers in most ways. They just had nine to five jobs. They drank, smoked, and used just as much, if not more, drugs than the hustlers that I was familiar with. One of the first things I learned at an early age is that everyone is a liar and a thief. It is just what you lie about and

18

what you steal. There are no exceptions. At the store, I worked for a man named Ron, who was the hardest working man that I have ever met. Ron was a dedicated family man and helped to formulate my work ethic. Ron was a special man, and his store was the meeting place for the hood.

There were pool tables, pinball machines, and a lounge area for people to congregate. People would spend their entire days in the store, and this became another chapter of my education in life. Ron had a "credit system" for his customers, and most of the customers had accounts. Most of these customers would pay on time, and it was very important for us to keep an accurate record because, for them, every penny counted. While you would think that these customers would be purchasing milk, bread, and other necessities, the primary items that they sought credit for included beer, cigarettes, and Big Red and Big Blue the illegal numbers papers. You have to remember I was barely a teenager, and I was thrust in a position to deal with adults. At times, Ron would run errands and leave me to man the store, and I would handle it with no problem. In fact, some people looked at me as an adult and would tell me their problems and seek advice. I remember one day being at the store alone and Ms. Mary coming in and asking me whether she should leave her husband after a night of fighting. I replied without hesitation, "No, but maybe you both need a vacation." Life can be simple sometimes, and we never know it. People just want somebody to talk to, and in some of these cases, I served as that someone. I have had great conversations with children, and one of their biggest complaints is never being heard. Adults, for the most part, have never been good listeners. Many children are reluctant to approach adults because they know they will not be heard. I was the exact opposite because I was a child being exposed to an adult world. I often hear people talk about their childhoods, and in most cases, that means doing kid stuff. I do not have many stories like that because I hung out with adults most of my life. My kid days were over before they ever really got going.

No matter how much time my brother and I spent in the streets, we always went to school. I was always a really good student, and that never changed throughout my life. I mastered doing my homework in school and would be early to school, no matter what happened the night before. Let me be clear. There were some nights when we would end up at home listening to music or watching corny shows like *Mary Tyler Moore* and *Carol Burnett*. This is what our world consisted of in the '70s. Years later, we would be introduced to *Sanford and Son*, *Good Times*, *Chico and the Man*, and other Black television. The irony is that Whites usually wrote these shows. While I will admit that some of it was funny, they still didn't really understand who we were. When Richard Pryor came along later, we really got a taste of people that I knew from the hood.

High school was an entirely different chapter in my life. In my neighborhood, most of us went to Springfield Gardens or August Martin, which were the local high schools. Living in New York City with a huge population, there are so many high schools available, so people from our neighborhood also went to schools where they had to take public transportation as well. At Springfield, we had split sessions, which meant either you went in early or late. During my first two years, I was not required to be in school until the afternoon, which gave me a lot of time to run around in the morning. My last two years were the exact opposite, where I finished school early and had the whole afternoon wide open. This is when my life really opened up for me. I had money coming from several sources, including selling weed and sometimes coke and running errands, including the illegal numbers for several of the older guys from my hood. In school, I also had great clientele, including some of the Whites who went to school with me. They had money regularly and a few teachers who liked to smoke weed. In our neighborhood, drugs were everywhere, so getting a package to sell was easy. My brother and I had great reputations, so everyone trusted us, and they were quick to put us on. As I got older, I did the same for a lot of younger cats, and in most cases, they did right by me as well. Being exposed to drugs and organized criminal activity taught me how to manage a business, and I would use those skills later in my life as a manager in corporate America.

In my teens, I was very popular in the hood wearing expensive clothing that most adults could not afford. I shopped at A.J. Lester, Leighton's, Phil Crownfields, Revel Knox, and Barneys when I got a little older. In most cases, I dressed way better than the adults that I came into contact with, including teachers, local businessmen, and parents. I can remember meeting parents of people I hung out with, and they would know right away that I was living differently than their son or daughter. They would ask me questions and, at times, be hesitant to have me around, but at the end of the day, I did well in school and was well mannered, two traits that impressed them. My brother and I were known for having shoes, especially sneakers. There were times when people would come to our home just to see our sneaker collection. Even though I do not like to go here, but material things really matter more in poorer communities. This is very sad and hasn't changed much since my teen years.

I was very mature as a teen because I spent most of my time around adults. I knew then, and still know now, when to keep my mouth shut and when to leave. In fact, one of my closet friends (Homie) still kids me today because he never knew when to leave, and it has cost him dearly. People in my neighborhood were getting money, and they were making sure that I did as well. Even though I made good money in the street, I also kept my job, which ensured that I would have the ability to keep up the lifestyle that I started. I usually hung out with older people, and this made me more popular with people my own age. One of the people who took me under his wing was Eddie B. Eddie was one of the coolest motherfuckers who ever lived. Ed was a neat freak like me, so we clicked immediately. Ed was two years older than I was. He was mixed, half Black and half Puerto Rican. Ed's family moved to Queens from Harlem, and he came from a big family. His mother remarried and had two more children, and Eddie was the baby from the first marriage. Ed was very well dressed, and most women thought he was very handsome. Ed

21

kept his afro shaped up at all times, and his sneakers were always spotless. At that time, he was one of the few people I had met who was neater than I was. When I met Ed, my life really changed because I would spend all of my time around adults except for my participation in sports. Ed's two children, Tia and Eddie Jr., are very special to me. They remind me of their father in certain ways and have grown into fine adults. Eddie is a former NBA player who made his father proud even though the credit should go their mother, Debbie. Deb, as we call her, saw a lot being around all of us, and I mean a lot. She was very strong, and all of us loved her dearly. She was the sister none of us had and still holds that position. I love you, DD. Again, no matter what happened at night, I went to school the next day. I cannot emphasize that more to young people that you must complete a certain level of education to have any chance in this world. Shortly after meeting Ed, I met Little True and then Civilized. True and Civ were real hustlers, and my experiences around them introduced me to the hard-core drug world. True and Civ spent a lot of time on the "Block" (a designated block in South Jamaica), where drugs were sold all day long. I would meet other close friends at this time as well and build some relationships that have lasted a lifetime. At this time, I still never had any experiences in using drugs, and my experiences were relegated to assisting and observing drugs in the hood. I would spend time with True and Civ, and they would always make sure I kept some money in my pocket. Ed, True, and Civ were best friends and were very protective of me. I was the young brother who went everywhere but still was not allowed to participate in all activities. While I am not advocating criminal behavior, I will say that when we came up, older brothers took their time to explain the streets to you. This was important because, in some cases, it even kept some people away from the lifestyle. When you did decide to go for it, you were much better prepared. While I was the baby in the older crew, I was the leader of the younger crew. Bill, Cal, Ben, Rick, Junie, and others were part of a crew that made some real loot and had a whole lot of fun. We were a special group of friends who trusted each other and watched each other's backs. You don't see that today; imagine real friends telling on each other like they do today. That never would happen in my era. While Ed and Civ have died, True and I remain best friends and still spend a lot of time together. For my younger crew, most have mixed reviews at this point in their lives. All have survived the challenges, including prison, alcoholism, drug addiction, and other issues affecting us all.

Word travels fast in the hood, and soon I was introduced to Rad. Rad was a major hustler who, at the time, had just finished serving time for some big deals that went bad. Rad was from Harlem and twelve years older than I was, but like we were attracted to him, he was attracted to us as well. Rad was the oldest of his brothers, a tough group of men who took no shit from anybody. Rad took me under his wing, and this meant spending a lot of time late-night uptown in Harlem and going on runs throughout the city. My education was quick and thorough. Rad always made sure I went to school, and this even meant getting dropped off in the morning right in front of the school. I would be dead tired but understood this was the price to pay for being in the streets. Years later, I would put my little brother Ben through the same lifestyle, something I am not proud of, but we both made it through. I can remember getting out of the car one morning after running with Rad and Ed all night, knowing I had a game that evening after school. I went to every class and took care of my other business, knowing that I could not lie down, or I would be done for the day. I played decently but knew that I needed to get my rest on days like that, or it would catch up to me. When the game was over, Rad, Ed, Jimbo, and the others from the hood really blasted me. They made it clear that there were no excuses and that if you shuffle, you deal, meaning that if you chose to run with the big boys, then this is what goes with it. I spent a lot of late hours in clubs and after-hours spots with Rad, Jimbo, Ed, True, Civ, and some others. I was a teenager in an adult world, and it prepared me for my adult life. I saw many of the so-called well-respected adults in my community using drugs, abusing alcohol, and doing other things that I feel no need to mention. It changed my perception of life. Here it was, these pillars and leaders of the community were no better than the people they looked down on.

In my mid-teens, I started selling cocaine for Rad, and that was the beginning of my hard-core street life. I spent a great deal of time on Guy R. Brewer until the wee hours of the night with all kinds of customers. We had late-night spots that never closed, and I had easy access to them all. For gambling, we had Rob's Garage, where some of the biggest gamblers in the city would come. Next to Rob's was Jimbo's, which was a spot that never closed where all the hustlers stayed waiting to earn a dollar. Jimbo was from West Virginia and had migrated to New York City. He worked for Scotty but was very close to Rad and sold everything, and I mean everything, from his spot. Jimbo supported many of the athletes from the hood, and he, Rad, Rob, and some of the others would always come to our games. Down the block from Jimbo's was Ms. Tweety's and Ms. Minnie Bells, who both ran the local whorehouses, which were always busy. I had a great relationship with both and often ate there and spent time with the girls who were great customers, but I was not a customer, lol.

I spent a great deal of time in them, all usually selling my product and running errands for people. An old hustler named Ed Wise told me, "Good men do bad things," and I never forgot that. Ed Wise would take me down to the Welfare Office and have me act as his son. He was a heavy heroin user (shooter) and only dated White women but a good hustler. He had access to all kinds of pills, and he would give me what I needed to sell because I had White customers in school who liked that high. Years later, I would assist Ed in a very tough situation. He died of an overdose not too long after that. Another character was Fleetwood, who was also a major dealer that Rad introduced me to. I was trained to go on major pickups by Rad and would accompany him as his right hand for many years. Fleetwood found out about it, and the next thing I know, I was accompanying him as well. Rad put a stop to that after a while, but I understood. I was making some good extra money, but it was a major risk. I was also high as a kite during these travels. Even though I always had weed, I was not a heavy smoker. My drug of choice was cocaine, which I liked with Remy Martin, a vice I learned from some of the people I was getting high with. I was heavily involved in basketball, so I was not high often and only drank when I used coke; but when I did get high, I went in.

I was raised by my mother to look for the good in people, and I have never deviated from that. Believe me, there have been times when I had to dig pretty deep for some of the people who I have met along the way.

Another person who was a big product of my early life was El Sun (John Dean). El Sun was a ghetto superhero. El was the person who they made the saying "would give you the shirt off of his back" for. El spent his late teenage years in prison. When he came home, he was breathing fresh air for us all. El was arguably the best athlete (other than Calvin Bruton) that I have ever seen. El was well-liked by both men and women. There were times when El would come up with huge sums of money and would share his wealth with the whole hood. We would all have new sneakers and money to eat with. El was very close to my brother and me, and when he died, it really hurt a lot of people. When El became ill his wife Sharon Coffee Dean stood by his side and took exceptional great care of him. This was an example of a woman who cared deeply for a man and it was shown in her actions. She is a special person with great character and I will always admire her and her family. Sharon you are big in my book. Will always love you.

One night, our team BLVD House won a very competitive basketball tournament at Christ the King, the local gym, and El sponsored a party at Jimbo's that we still talk about until this day. Jimbo, Rad, Rob, Yap Yap, Buddy, Ronnie G., and all of the old-time hustlers came to see us play every week, and it made us all feel good. See, again, the hustlers thought more about the youths than some of the community leaders and other men in the hood. I will make this clear as day for you. Your child may be the worst player on the team or the least talented in the school play. They still want to see you in the audience. Most of us did not have fathers, and our mothers were involved in our lives already, so we needed men. The only men who cared about us were the men in the street. The difference today is the quality of men in the streets has diminished. Many of the men today are in no position to teach anyone. We were kept in line by unwritten rules that people took seriously. Education was always going on, and we were eager to learn. We were all good listeners and had respect for our elders, no matter if they were a money-making hustler or someone who was going through hard times. The very few times one of the younger guys got out of line, the other OGs would step in to ensure that respect remained for their peers. I still miss Famers and New York (Guy R. Brewer), but wow, you have changed.

Red Light, Green Light, 123 – Growing up in New York City was a challenge for many of us in the '70s. You have to remember the drinking age was eighteen and you could also get into the clubs as well. New York City was grimy during this era with peep shows, open prostitution, teenage drinking and drug usage, and unprotected sex. What you witness today, with campaigns promoting condoms and safe sex, was not available during this era. Many of my friends, both male and female, became teenage parents. In addition, many of us started getting high on weed, cocaine, and alcohol. When I got to middle school, a few older students were experimenting with dope (heroin). Most sniffed dope (heroin), but there were a few who skin-popped, and we would stand guard at the bathroom door while they got off. I had watched my cousin, Harry, who was significantly older than I was, do this earlier in my life, so I was not shocked to see this, and after a while, it was normal behavior in some circles. I vowed I would never touch heroin, and I never did. This does not make me a hero, though, because I made up for it with my cocaine use in the late '70s and early '80s. Cocaine had become the drug of choice at this time after being thought of as a rich person's drug earlier in the decade.

During my travels, I met a lot of people who would be my friends for life, but my life was getting ready to change for the worse. In 1978, after I graduated high school, I was on top of the world. I was scheduled to attend college in Pennsylvania in September to play basketball, but when I arrived with two of my closet friends (Mike and Nick), everything was not what we expected. Please keep in mind that we had prepared for this all year training and perfecting our games and dominating the summer tournaments, but when we got to the school, we faced some obstacles that we were not prepared for. The first thing was that we would be in direct competition with the guys from Philly who had the upper hand on us because the upper classmates on the team were from Philly. When we went to the gym to work out, we had to go head to head against them, and after the first day, they knew we were no joke. We formed friendships with some others from New York City, and from that day on, we stuck together. When practices started, we were ready, and we all played well and even handled ourselves well against the upperclassman. We were shocked later to find out that the coach had the guys from Philly higher than us on the depth chart. This really blew us away, and we lost our desire to play. After the semester was over, we were out of there. In hindsight, it was probably not the best move, but I was homesick, and there was nobody to talk me out of leaving. I could not call my mother and tell her my predicament; she would have said to me, "Nigga, figure it out," and I wouldn't blame her at all. When I got home in just a short time, some things had changed, for one, Rad, and others were not happy to see me back. All of my money sources had vanished, and it would be a while before I would recover. I was no longer in high school, and my mother was not going to provide any financial assistance to me for the apartment. She said, "You want to be grown, be grown." This was different for me because, while in high school, I had money from different sources, and she would hit me off here and there because she did still keep things in the apartment, but that was over. I hit the streets running and eventually found a job at a major manufacturing corporation in Long Island City. This job was perfect for me. I operated a printing press and delivered blueprints to the construction sights. Once I learned how things worked, I created my own system where I would come in early and make all of the blueprints and then spend the rest of the day delivering the prints to the job sites. They loved me here because my system worked perfectly because the site managers always had the changes early in the day. We got paid on Mondays, which in the beginning was a pain in the ass for me, but after a while, that was also perfect for me. I laid really low, barely coming out for a while because I was embarrassed and only going to work. After a couple of months, I had some money and went to Rad and some others after I had some money to make some moves. They welcomed me back with some long lectures for months, but I took it like a man. Immediately, I got me some work, and between the job and reclaiming some customers, I was back on my feet. However, there was one difference I was sniffing coke more frequently and started to slip in some other ways as well. I still had the apartment, but there was more traffic in and out because, in the drug game, you never know when you are going to make a sale. I had a great connection now and was able to have some weighty customers, which meant more money, but in my case, I was not as sharp as before, and the money was leaving my hands as fast as I could earn it. I still bought clothes and looked great, but I could feel something bad was coming my way. The first sign was that our landlord, Aunt Ruth (what we called her), had contacted my mother and told her that her daughter would like to take the apartment very shortly. Very shortly was in sixty days. I had also given a very close friend some weight on credit, and he got knocked (arrested), and this really put me in a big hole. So, now I was looking at having nowhere to live and had lost some much-needed money. So, I am nineteen years old with a chippie (like to sniff coke, but not a habit), short on money, and with no experience in finding a place to live. Those sixty days went by so fast for me. I asked my job for a raise, and they told me they would give me a quarter more an hour. I was so angry I quit the next week—another bad decision. During this time, my mother went through a life-changing auto accident and was hospitalized for an extended period. Besides, I would never have told her anything I was going through. I was grown early in my teens. This was not time to revert back to being a child. As the clock ticked for me, I became more confused, and for the first time in my life, I was scared.

I was able to store my personal belongings at various friends' houses during this period, which took some pressure off. But there were some nights I had nowhere to go. I was very proud and didn't want to ask my friends every night if I could stay, so I often lied about where I stayed. There were some nights I would stay in Jimbo's or Ms. Mary's until the sun came up and then go to a friend's house for a shower and change my clothes. There were a couple nights I even slept on the train after walking around Manhattan. This was my reality. I was a young man who had navigated the streets to a point where everything came crashing down. I was lost but proud. I had some money, and with all of the clothes that I had, I could fool everybody, but some of those nights it was really scary for me.

After a period of being lost, the Crutch family saved me. Benjamin Sr. and Doris Crutch were the parents of Cheryl and Ben Jr. Ben Jr. (four years younger than I was) had become our little brother for Tim and me, and we had become extremely close. Before we lost the apartment, Ben Jr. spent a lot of time with us, and we still share that bond. The Crutches opened their home to my brother and me and treated us better than anyone ever has. Their kindness saved my life at a time that I could have easily ended up in prison or worse. There is not a day that goes by that I do not think of the support and love they extended to me. I owe them so much, and it bothers me at times that I have not been in a position to do more for them. They are amazing people who assisted so many of us over the years. Thank you again for being there for me. I truly love you with all of my heart.

After this period, I also had a stay with my brothers, Mike and Gary Cooper. Their mother, Momma Frances, also was very good to me and always treated me as her son. I was, and still am, close with the Cooper brothers. I look at them as my blood family. We have been through so much together, and they were also there for me in my toughest times.

After this period, my uncle found out about my situation, and he reached out to me to live with his family in Woodside Projects on the other side of the city. I have a big family, based mostly in Georgia, but my uncle and his wife, my Aunt Kate, who were from Georgia, had lived in New York for a significant amount of time. Their children, Lenoris, Nan, and Bernard, were the only people in my family who my brother and I had regular contact with. When we were younger, we would spend weekends with them, and we always got along. It never crossed my mind to reach out to them, but once a got there, I fit right in. Uncle PoBoy (Cooper) and Aunt Kate were churchgoing, hardworking people who always treated my brother and me very well. Aunt Kate always had plenty of food and made sure I ate well while my uncle, who is very quiet, allowed me to move, as I wanted to. I never gave them any cause for concerns and was relieved to have a consistent place to live. I made the apartment a little crowded, but no one ever complained. They also played a big role in me getting my feet on the ground, and I enrolled in college again at this time, approaching my twentieth birthday. I had slowed down a bit but still made my regular trips to South Jamaica to get some money and stay connected.

Community college in New York City was better than I thought with a very diverse group of students. The campus was very new and was literally fifteen minutes via train from our apartment, and I knew a lot of people already. My reputation had preceded me. The kicker was that Rad, who had actually graduated from the school years before, was working in the "Student Affairs Department." This was good and bad for me. Before the semester with his direction, I was making sales with ease. This was cake for me because I was not looking over my shoulder for stick up kids or police. In addition, I was going to school. Selling drugs on campus was ideal for somebody like me who knew how to navigate the streets and different scenarios. I was still a good student, and college was easy for me except for "statistics," which was hell. My brother, Mike, was with me, and in a very smooth way, we established ourselves to both of the women and men who were drawn to us for the way we dressed and carried ourselves. Between classes, we would pop into Rad's office and check in. Sometimes, he would refer us to customers, and somedays we would even get high. We didn't go overboard, but it was like a big party. I even became president of one of the student government organizations through Rad's direction, which connected me to a whole new base of customers. I went back to the hood and talked with some of my friends who were hustling on the block and told them that this was a better hustle.

The gym was relatively new, and I started playing ball regularly, spending time on campus. There was a rivalry with guys from other boroughs on the courts, but the crew we had from Queens was tough, and we won several tournaments. I was easy to find hanging close to the gym, which was close in proximity to the cafeteria. A lot of guys from other areas started seeking me out, and the money was good, especially when the students got refund checks. I was just not selling recreationally anymore with others looking to buy weight. I even had guys from Washington Heights coping, which was strange because they had it good up there. The New York Knicks practiced at the school, and before you knew, a couple of them were my best customers. They would even leave me tickets at the will-call window.

Eventually, I went on a college internship at the Exxon Corporation, which was very exciting for a twenty-one-year young Black man with my background. Keep in mind, I had very good grades was very disciplined in most ways. At Exxon, you had to wear a suit and tie every day, and I loved it. I already had a lot of clothes, and this gave me the opportunity to wear the suits I had and buy more. My previous experience at my first corporate job paid immediate dividends. The White hierarchy did not intimidate me, and I was very articulate. I learned my responsibilities quickly and received great reviews. The pay was great, and at twenty-one years of age, I was gaining enormous experience. I was very disappointed when the internship ended, but I knew I had to return to school and finish my other requirements. Again, I picked up some customers, and many of them were with me long after leaving Exxon. Lol.

After a sketchy period, I found myself spending more and more time back in my old hood in South Jamaica. During this period, money was coming in, and we had established a great network. We started to get careless, which meant spending a lot of time hanging out and staying up all night. We would take cabs everywhere and sponsor coke parties. One of my partners, Dre, fell into the dope world, and it consumed him. Once he started sniffing heroin, he couldn't stop and remains in that condition today. He was a superstar hustler who drove women crazy with his looks and charm. Later, he would spend long periods in prison and never reached his potential. When I see him, I always tell him I love him, but it hurts to see him and what he has become.

Then, there is Homie, who I cannot speak much about because of different reasons. We became very close in this period (the early '80s) after forming a brotherhood in our teens. Our late-night conversations on Malcolm and Martin are legendary. He was and still is the most driven person I have ever met and is still one of the most respected people from the streets ever. There were times we worked together in the streets, but for the most part, he did his thing, and we did ours. Besides, I was my own boss, something that he respected then and now. During this period, we would spend a lot of time together while he rebuilt his life and built his reputation. Homie could have done anything he wanted to in life, and contrary to what some might think, still can play a role in reaching the streets, something that many others have failed to do.

In the early '80s, one of my little brothers, Junie, was fatally shot in the streets. At this time, we all were going full blast, spending long hours in the street. Junie has a tremendous amount of heart, and even though he was short, he would try anybody. Junie was a hell of an athlete and a really good basketball player. If he would have gone to school and avoided the streets, he could have really gone far with his game. Knowing what I know now, I probably would have intervened a little more when I saw him moving a little too fast. Junie recovered from the shots to his head and body, and although he lost most of his sight, he regained his mental capacity and his body movements. It was a miracle, and even after everything he had been through, he never complained and refused to take sympathy from anybody. He is alive and well, and his mind is sharp as ever. Our families are close, and we continue to have the big brother-little brother relationship today. When Junie went through this experience, it affected all of us, and we all took life more seriously and became more focused.

In the early '80s, the drug game was changing, and so was cocaine. That change was the "base," which was the mother of crack. Freebase cocaine is the process of "freeing" the cocaine base from its natural salt form, resulting in pure cocaine. Inhaled freebase cocaine results in an immediate and intense high. Once it enters the bloodstream through the lungs, the person experiences feelings of euphoria and an extreme high. These feelings last for approximately thirty minutes before the person experiences a crash. And boy did they crash. Crack cocaine came later and was cheaper and more available and destroyed our community and many others, but freebasing got it all going. I can remember spending weekends in customer's houses while they would continue to purchase coke to cook it up and free base. We made a lot of money and would have made even more, but the banks closed on Friday at 3:00 pm in the early '80s so people could not get to their money until Monday morning, so it saved some people. Others would part with family heirlooms, offer TVs, VCRs, and other appliances, turn to prostitution, or even worse, rather than crash. I watched some pretty pitiful situations and slowly but surely it eroded away my money-first mentality. This period lasted for me for a while, and I eventually ended up living in Brooklyn with my future wife, Toni, and mother of my children, traveling to South Jamaica to hustle in the daytime. I still would end up with Homie and others hanging out at times, but I had matured a lot in a short period. I did not want to continue to take chances and wanted to avoid prison. Toni was also not making it easy for me and was putting the pressure on me to get out of the game. There were times I had drugs in my possession when I had my children with me. This did not happen often, but it happened. I am somewhat embarrassed now when I think of these times, but it was my reality. Please, hustlers, be careful what you do around your children. They are smarter and more observant than you think. I had an exit plan but wanted to gather as much money as possible. I already had one daughter, and a baby was on the way. While we had our own place to live, I knew that Toni expected more from me, which included a better place to live. While I kept doing my thing, I also got a night job at UPS, which I hated. I literally got no sleep and did this nonstop for about four months. During this period, I also would get the *NY Times* and research the help wanted section in hopes of securing a job in Manhattan. I had the opportunity to taste working in the city, and I missed it. Dressing up every day and venturing into the city was exciting to me, and I already had experience from Exxon and my first job.

I also reached a major milestone during this period. The weekend of my twenty-third birthday, I celebrated having a great time, and I promised myself that after that night, I would never sniff coke again. I have kept that promise. I did not have to enter a program or seek assistance from anybody. I made up my mind, and that is what I did. Let me be clear. I am not putting myself on a pedestal. From sixteen to twenty-three, I partied and lived a very fast life that included sniffing coke. I also started some people on sniffing coke the same way people brought me into that same world. I apologize from the bottom of my heart to those people; you know who you are. If you know, you know! I know that does not mean a lot right now, but I wanted to say it. I strongly advise people not to start getting high, especially from coke or dope (heroin). Most never recover, especially women. Some of the things I was involved in, I have to deal with for the rest of my life, and although I can handle it, I am impacted by these experiences. In part, that is why I have volunteered so much of my time to helping people in my hood. The drug game is a beast that most are just not built for. I was disciplined and was able to eventually put my life back together. I was driven and wanted to be there for my future wife and children. Many in my crew were not as fortunate, and drugs have impacted their lives for many years. I will always be loyal to them all and have always made myself available if needed. Although I kept hustling, I also started selling weight in weed, which would eventually take me away from coke. The weed did well for me and allowed me more time to focus on finding a job and establishing my youth program. I still had one foot in the street and would for many years after that, but I had matured and was looking to do well in life.

I do not give a fuck what some people have to say on the subject of street hustlers being a valuable component in turning our communities around. There are millions of young people involved in the streets who can turn it around and become valuable in their communities. Don't let people view you as useless. Develop an "exit plan" for getting out of the streets. Clean yourself up, get in shape, do your research, and make it happen. Seek out mentors from the streets who have turned it around in your hood and ask for help. You have to come right and be respectful. If you can't find somebody, I got you in whatever way I can.

Many of the hustlers would have done well in the business world if they had not gotten caught up in the streets. The streets, particularly in a city like New York, can be overwhelming. You finally get the opportunity to make some money and think you are on top of the world. The sad part is that you are one felony away from a tough life with limited chances. As a teenager, I was really amazed at how much money was being made. The flip side was how many families were being destroyed. Prison is not a deterrent to the streets when life is already tough. Everyone aspires for a better life, and for many of us, we do not believe that we will attain it just going to school. The educational system needs a major overhaul if we expect to create change. More funding needs to be allocated to flexible education programs that will include ex-convicts, street hustlers, and addicts. I will be very clear there are some people with criminal records who can do a much better job than a lot of these college graduates with experience. At the end of the day, many of these people have real-life experience and common sense, which beats that piece of paper and nepotism. There is a deep fear that people, particularly Black and Hispanic, can actually return to society and be productive. The bottom line is that prisons are very lucrative, and the only way they stay that way is to keep them full.

When I look at Homie, True, Civ, Yap, Rad, Jimbo, Ed Wise, and many others who I spent time with in the streets, I see people who could have accomplished so much if they had been mentored and truly believed in education as it was introduced in the schools. In many areas, we all were very organized and understood protocol such as "chain of command," "business hierarchy," product and demand," and marketing. Everyone had their own way of marketing their products and established their own banking systems, including credit and cash loans. I would meet some people at this time of my life who today still remain very close to me. Homie is a street legend who many people really never understood. He was arguably the best businessperson I ever met but caught up in the game so much that he got swallowed up. Many youngsters are still trying to emulate his legend, but really don't understand the price that he has paid. Hopefully, he will get his chance to prove his worth. There is not a doubt in my mind that he can make a difference for many in the streets.

Last, shortly after my twenty-third birthday, I ended up with a management trainee position in Manhattan and a new apartment in Rochdale Village in my hood just before my second daughter was born.

New York City Basketball – Growing up in New York City, you could never get enough of the "city game." Basketball is like religion in New York City. I know some other places that turn out some great talent, but New York City is a special place for basketball. In my time, I saw and played with some great players. Not every one of them went to the NBA. Some didn't even go to college, but if you know basketball, then you know that with it being so competitive that you need to have some luck to get the opportunity to make it to the NBA.

In the '70s, the best basketball was played in the New York City parks both in tournaments and in pick-up games. It was no big deal to see the best players in the city, putting their talent on display at either. Good players would travel from park to park challenging players from that area. There were rarely any fights despite how rough the play might get. The common rule was no blood, no foul, and real players accepted it within reason. I can remember playing in some games that truly tested your resolve. Many players took great pride in playing defense, which is clearly missing today. Shooting is also a lost art; while in the '60s '70s and '80s, many of us could shoot and use the backboard with regularity. We all took great pride in free throw shooting. Many games were decided at the line, and it was not uncommon to see many of us in the park late at night practicing our free throws. The difference then was that we would schedule time to practice each day and then still make it to the party.

Today, I would be labeled as a fair-weather Knicks fan. I would not argue because the teams that they have chosen to me do not represent New York City basketball. The greatest teams of all time, in my opinion, are still the Knicks championship teams of 1969 and 1973. These teams included Walt Frazier, Willis Reed, Dave Debushere, Bill Bradley, Dick Barnett, Cazzie Russell Mike Riordan, Phil Jackson, later in '73, Earl Monroe and Jerry Lucas. For the most part, all of these guys were great individual players who sacrificed their games for the benefit of the team. Earl and Clyde were the best guards of their era, excluding Jerry West, and they learned to play together and complement each

38

other. That is a testimony to teamwork, something that is taken for granted in sports and, most of all, in life. Again, young people remember that life is a team sport, and no one wins without the assistance of others.

As I look at the current team of the Knicks, I see a corporation that really doesn't care as long as they continue to make a profit. The question is, do they really understand what it is to win a championship in New York City? I doubt it when I see some of the things they do off of the court. Before you can do reality shows, commercials, and hang out late at clubs, win something. I know you have a right to do as you please with your money and time but be ready for the public to come at you in New York City. We are not an ordinary city and demand more from everyone that comes here. Don't whine or look for sympathy from us. The flip side of this is if you do win a championship, we will treat you like royalty. For example, Clyde, Earl, Willis, Joe Namath, Reggie Jackson, Derek Jeter, Darryl Strawberry, LT, Phil Simms, the list goes on and on of former players who are still appreciated for winning a championship in the Big Apple. I love the work the NBA players are doing off the court. Lebron James, Dwayne Wade, Carmello Anthony, Chris Paul, Kevin Durant, Steph Curry, Jimmy Butler, and some others are really committed to social change. They recognize they have power and have the common sense to know they have children growing up in this world. I hope they pull their resources together and start their own league. I am so impressed with them venturing out into other fields and taking power from the establishment. They are creating "maps" for success for the young people of color. I salute you, my young brothers.

I dedicated a chapter of the book to basketball because I strongly believe that basketball in New York City and other big cities (Chicago, LA, Philadelphia, Detroit, Atlanta, Houston, and others) is responsible for a lot of the success of Black men. I don't think that we know how to get the most out of things that work. If you were to stop and look at one of the largest factors that get Black men to college, it would be basketball and other sports. Instead, we allow others to label us as just athletes or jocks. Fuck that! Use your talents to get into school and take advantage of the opportunity. Never apologize for using your talent, no matter what people say. In some cases, basketball and other sports have kept some of us from prison. I am a prime example of someone who was always involved in basketball, which kept my life on a schedule with games and practices. The fact that I was committed to the game separated me from my closest friends who had no activities to occupy their time. When I would have games or practices, they would be involved in illegal activity, and sometimes things went wrong. There was a brief time in my early twenties when I was really hustling hard and lost myself for a minute. I had a meeting with myself and figured out what was missing in my life. It was sports, particularly basketball. I got back into shape and started working with kids again and have not stopped since. It was simple. I just needed a minute to figure it all out. My secret to life has always been to stay around young people providing guidance and leadership. My organization, R.I.S.E., has enabled me to do so. I have always had a gym to use because I made it a priority, and so can you. It won't be easy, and sometimes you will have to create ways to pay for it, but from what I hear, some of you are getting it like that.

Experts from various fields will point out that we should be able to excel in academics without sports being involved similar to other cultures, but the bottom line is that Black men and sports are inseparable. We are more talented in sports than any other culture, and because of that, we will continue to pursue the dream. The flip side to this is that we have to create a curriculum that embraces sports and, at the same time, makes our youths understand the importance of education. We haven't done that yet. I have organized basketball programs at 5:00 am and have gotten participation from some of the most so-called undisciplined youths that have ever lived. The difference is that they love the game, and two, they know I am not full of shit. So, from this, I am saying that we need to use basketball (sports) as an enticement to get them disciplined and, from there, push your academic agenda. We tend to do it the other way around, and it fails. We lose kids, and those kids return to the streets. Instead, if we would have customized our curriculum to the youths, we have a much better chance for success. Again, I know I will get detractors that will argue that we should not have to sacrifice academics for sports, but these are some of the same fools who can't wait to serve on a jury and send someone to prison.

I will emphasize this point again. Many of the men that I grew up with, including myself, are not in prison today because of sports and primarily basketball. There were some nights that I would have been in a car or on a corner, but I had a game or practice and did not participate in criminal activity because of this. Anybody who grew up in New York City or any urban area will tell you that criminal activity is always around, and if you are not busy, there is a chance you will take part. Some of us even go along for the ride because, in many cases, we are loyal to friends. Some of the best basketball players that I have ever seen became criminals (according to your criteria) later in their lives due to the absence of basketball (sports) in their lives. I am not making excuses for them. In some cases, economics played a major role as well, but if they had a gym, a team, or some kids to coach and given a stipend, some of them would have found another way.

Instead, we continue to invest in prisons. Since I was eighteen years old, I always made sure that I had access to a space, gym, or recreation program that young people could be a part of. I knew that most young people would not be as street smart or have the commonsense level to stay clear from the lure of the streets. My foundation was built on basketball, and that was the cornerstone for an educational and recreational organization that has served over 50,000 unduplicated youths and adults for close to three decades. In all my years, I have never had a physical fight in our gym, never had to call the police (never would anyway), and rarely had to kick anyone out. I learned from some great men who cared that if you show love and affection to our children, they respond positively. We need to find qualified men and women to operate more recreational and educational

41

programs after normal school hours. We need to reevaluate many of the men and women who have served time in prisons and really give them a second chance. Some of these people have real-life experiences that are more valuable than what is learned in the classroom. Let me be clear. I am not talking about sexual offenders. Many of the programs and people who are operating the programs today are doing it solely for the dollar. This is killing our communities because they really don't care. Many of these organizations have the inside track to funding and are awarded year after year when it is clear they are not making a difference. Some of their staff are full of incompetent, poorly trained, losers who hide behind a college degree when, in fact, they have no clue how to deal with children of color, particularly Black and Hispanic. In some of these cases, they also are sexual predators that are feasting on our children. In our communities, we need to step up and take a close look at the programs and people that are serving our children and take action when it is necessary. If that means you have to cross the line to protect our children, then so be it. Enough said!

Higher Education – I have spent a great deal of time on college campuses, sometimes for the wrong reasons. I was always a very good student, and contrary to what most people think, my brother is more formally educated than I am. This is not a slap at my brother, but since I have done so many things in my life, people assume that I am this super college-educated family man. While I have probably spent more than enough time in college classrooms at various institutions, I always vacated for different reasons, including money, housing, and even confusion. Truth be told, I am an extremely well organized, very intelligent, self-educated former street hustler with a hell of a lot of common sense. I have attended several colleges but never completed my college education. I have been an avid reader my whole life, and while many of my peers were being trained in classrooms, I was studying James Baldwin, Richard Wright, Alex Haley, Dr. Henrik Clarke, Ivan Van Sertima, Langston Hughes, Walter Rodney, Frantz Fanon, George Jackson, and many more. While attending college at eighteen years old, I read *The Autobiography of Malcolm X* by Malcolm X and Alex Haley, and after that, my life was never the same. This book was special to me because Malcolm was so much like people I knew, including myself. He was someone who came from the streets and turned his life around. Malcolm said things that made sense and stood up for us without being pushed around. I loved Martin Luther King Jr., but most of the people I knew were more like Malcolm.

In today's society, attending and graduating college is extremely important. The training you receive and the access to resources will help you in your self-development. I strongly advocate going to college and finishing. It is even more important if you are Black and Hispanic. My college experiences, for the most part, were very pleasant. I had good intentions when I enrolled, but the life I was leading pushed me to utilize college for my financial benefit. I also was getting high regularly, like many of you are doing now. I am warning you; some of you will not recover from your drug use if you don't catch yourself before it is too late. You think you have it under control with oxycontin and other opioids, Adderall, heroin, and cocaine. Seek someone out to talk to and pull yourself together. You do not want to enter the working world with a drug problem, whether you work for yourself or somebody else. You will be exposed; trust me, the signs will present themselves. On a positive note, I spent a considerable amount of time at Howard University later in my life because two of my children attended Howard, and my youngest daughter attended Howard Law as well, so I had great experiences living vicariously through them. I attended many homecomings and spent a lot of time in Washington, D.C., a very special city. My middle daughter attended St John's, where she received a very vanilla education. In some ways, I think it helped her differently, and she has matured in some very special ways. She has a special way with children, and the experiences at this Catholic university smoothed her out for the long haul.

However, many of the graduates are not thinkers and, in some cases, are not prepared for life. These graduates come into the working world as robots and lack the common sense to make critical decisions. While they can function by applying their expertise to their field, many have problems in working with people. The ability to work and understand people is the greatest gift one can possess. I have witnessed many college graduates come into business environments and have no clue on how to deal with people. In some cases, they have been given managerial positions based simply on a degree and the color of their skin. This is an area where I have difficulty because the ability to manage requires more than a degree and skin color. You need the ability to make decisions, and this requires common sense. In many cases, some of these graduates just have none.

Some of the most intelligent people I know are not college-educated, and I would take them over some of you with your PhDs. Another issue that I have a problem with is the educational elitism that many of you wear like a badge. Just because you have that piece of paper does not mean that you are higher on the human totem pole than those who are less educated.

My three beautiful, educated daughters are not perfect, but the one thing they possess that many others do not is they have common sense. Since they were young, they have been a part of educational programs in the hood operated by R.I.S.E. as both participants and, in some cases, as coordinators. They collected food and clothing for shelters, attended teenage pregnancy programs, assisted with mentoring programs, organized trips, handed out literature, cleaned the parks, operated fundraisers, and spent time with what I like to call real people. As parents, my wife and I set goals, including *at least* a bachelor's degree, and they delivered. Our "plan" was based on forty-eight years of education, which measures sixteen years apiece. My youngest daughter finished early, so the goal was completed six months early. For your numbers, people, my wife and I were both forty-eight when the goal was completed. Later on, they returned to school and achieved even greater success. In addition, they have started their own businesses and have gained valuable experience managing assets and becoming outstanding parents to their children.

Let me be clear. College is not for everyone. Some of you in this technology, social-media-driven world, will succeed without college, but with the tools and resources available at some of these institutions, it is worth the investment. Just for the record, student loans are the biggest rip-off going. Try to find a way to get this done. I don't have all of the answers. If I could do it all over, I would have stayed in college the first time I went, but I was living in a "different world." Bison, you know!

45

R.I.S.E (Recreational Inner-city Sports and Education, Inc.) –
"To provide quality educational and recreational programming to inner-city youths that is designed to combat drug addiction, violence, teenage pregnancy, HIV and other STDs, and learning deficiencies. In addition, R.I.S.E. provides a positive environment that is fun, innovative, and safe for both participants and coordinators. All programs utilize a holistic approach that provides counseling, mentoring, and training that assists participants in becoming responsible adults. R.I.S.E. programs strive to empower participants with the goal to improve the community as a whole and provide hope for future generations."

"We Are Built for the Struggle"

R.I.S.E. is an acronym for Recreational Inner-City Sports and Education, Inc. R.I.S.E. is a nonprofit educational and recreational organization that provides quality programs for both youths and adults. R.I.S.E. was established in the early '80s, and since that time, it has provided services for thousands of participants. **Truth be told, R.I.S.E. is a very organized and experienced *grassroots organization* that masquerades as a community-based organization (CBO) when necessary.** A *grassroots* movement is one that uses the people in a given community as the basis for uplifting the community and its residents. Grassroots organizations use collective action from the people to effect change in the community. Grassroots organizations are associated with bottom-up, rather than top-down, decision making and are sometimes considered more natural or spontaneous than more traditional power structures. Grassroots organizations encourage community members to contribute by taking responsibility and action for their community. Grassroots organizations build power from the people and stay connected to the streets and, at times, use unconventional means to support its mission. Grassroots organizations work toward these and other goals via strategies that enlist the participation of people in the streets. Some grassroots organizations have no official listing but provide their community consistent, efficient results.

A community-based organization (CBO) is a private nonprofit organization that is representative of a community or significant segments of a community, which provides educational, recreational, vocational, rehabilitation, training, or internship programs and includes neighborhood groups and organizations, community action agencies, community development corporations, union-related organizations, employer-related organizations, and many others. CBOs can be big or small. While they are nonprofit, usually, the bulk of their budgets go to salaries, which at times, can be ineffective people. Many CBOs are well connected and receive funding from governmental sources, whether they are the best organization for the job or not. In some cases, the person making the decision looks like you and probably gets a kickback, which means money for favoring their organization. In many communities, this is why we continue to suffer because poorly managed CBOs that are not connected to the pulse of the community and with NO vested interest continue to receive contracts to repeat the same unsatisfactory work year after year. The CBOs submit written data to support their work to governmental agencies, which have no clue of the accuracy and sincerity of the reporting but accept it without hesitation, and this cycle continues for years and years. Usually, some of these bigger CBOs become the handpicked funding recipients of the funding sources and have to do little if anything to retain the funding. In some cases, you have smaller, more committed, and knowledgeable organizations that submit proposals for the funding that never have a chance. These organizations, in many cases, are grassroots organizations that do not have the connections of the bigger CBOs. For those of you political science majors, you are well aware that a successful grassroots movement can get you elected president, which many believe had a major impact on Obama's successful run.

The funding for R.I.S.E. came from various sources, including city, state, and federal government, private foundations, and private donors. Some years, we received pretty decent funding from the governmental agencies. Proposal writing was one of my strong suits, and we submitted quality proposals consistently. We

47

have assisted hundreds of organizations over the years in writing, preparing, and submitting proposals. We were honest in this respect to budgets and only requested funding that we would actually utilize. We also received outside funding from various sources that enabled us to provide services that really made a difference in the community. We had a funding system where we find an independent funder to directly pay a vendor for us for goods and services. We did not need to touch the money. We would have an independent funder sponsor a kid directly, especially when they were on their way to college. That's right, NCAA, you bastards. This system was extremely effective, and for some of our funders, they found some worth in their lives for assisting us. We did not judge people for their lives. We accepted them, and they accepted us. Our long track record of providing services to the community built trust, and we continue to have that today. We just found a way to keep providing programs. What I have learned over the years is that organizations that can really make a difference will never receive large amounts of funding or face obstacles on how to use the funding. I have witnessed time and time again, organizations that come into our communities and provide inadequate programs and continue to receive lucrative contracts. Many of these organizations, or at least the leadership, are not Black or brown people. These organizations take the majority of the funding and allocate it to salaries and benefits while our communities continue to suffer. Many of the people on the staff of these organizations are not committed to the uplift of people in struggle and view their role as a job and nothing more. Like many teachers and other educators, they take the check and run. Take a look at many of the organizations that provide services to inner-city youths and make a valid attempt to see if they are making a difference. Many of these organizations lack the expertise that is necessary to create positive change. They spend years in our communities, and their only requirement is to submit reports with data to their funders, which is useless when it comes to real-life circumstances. Let me be clear. Reporting can be useful if you have a real understanding of the people you are reporting about. Most of these organizations do not. The bullshit starts from the beginning when the request for proposal is issued, and most of the decision-makers already know who will be allocated funding and who will not. They allow a couple of no-names to obtain a few dollars, but the big bucks continue to go to the same organizations that continue to deceive us. Recently, in New York City, we witnessed politicians allocate funding to dummy organizations, and when they were caught, everybody just swept it under the rug. Do you really believe this was something new? The other sad reality is that we have a lot of our own people in cahoots with these bastards. They sell our children out and then smile in our faces.

The difference with us at R.I.S.E. is that if we discovered one of our people selling out the community, they would pay the price. I remember in the early '80s, there was a certain principal who made it clear that he would do whatever he wanted and didn't care what the community thought. Parents, teachers, and students felt disrespected. We scheduled a meeting and tried to resolve the issue peacefully, and he just didn't get it. Our next step was to deliver a message that he would understand, and he resigned right after that. While some will argue with our methods, there are times when you need to get things done, and there was no time to waste. Black men need to be more active in their communities and be ready to take action for positive change when necessary. There will be resistance, especially in schools where they really do not want the presence of Black men. They have instituted a model for many schools to make them resemble prisons. They are trying to prepare our children for prison. In some communities, we have positive Black and Hispanic men who would love to be a part of the education process, not as teachers or administrators, but as counselors and mentors. We need to be spending on programs that would train them and make them part of the solution instead of constantly portraying them as villains. I have been to some of the most so-called toughest hoods in the world and met some of the most committed people.

Chairman Dr. Bernard Gassaway, CFO Roger King, and I as president/executive director lead R.I.S.E. Others who have played major roles on the board include my childhood friend, Curtis Spaulding, Ken Bastian, Lance Lilly, Corey Jones, Richard Anderson, Mike Cooper, and my family. There have been some very dedicated and committed individuals who have been instrumental in making R.I.S.E. the special organization it is, including Greg Crosby (set the groundwork), Jeff Jones, George Williams, Raymond Smith, Bob Harwell, Craig Kat Keyes, William Billy Wright, Tim Clifton, David Reed, Faye Feller, Ron Gardner, Vivien Carter, Linda Saul (RIP), Anthony Roper, Mike Booker, Laron Mapp, Miguel Gonzalez, Ronald Yates, Donald Wright, Erica Ford, Laron Mapp, Ronald Yates, Wes Nelson, Daon Merritt, Derrick Germany, Larry Cave, and Jermaine Miller (RIP). These individuals and many more put in a lot of quality time attempting to make life better for many disadvantaged people. R.I.S.E. is an organization built on volunteers. Our staff consists of volunteers who are committed to positive change. We are an organization that, for the majority of our existence, never paid salaries. The money we raised went directly to our programs and the people. This separated us from many organizations where it is the exact opposite where the majority of their funds went to salaries.

Since R.I.S.E. was started, I have worked with some very committed individuals. Ken Bastian was an Army veteran who I met one day on the train. Ken had served all over the world and brought a different approach to dealing with people. Ken would not take no for an answer and was instrumental in working with the local politicians and clergy. There were times Ken would drive me crazy, but I knew he would do anything for the organization and me. Ken became very close to my family and spent a lot of time in my home. I consider him my brother, and even though he has moved to another state, we remain close.

Roger King was someone I knew from the hood. Roger's specialty was finance. One day, I approached Roger about working with us, and the rest is history. Roger immediately took charge of our financial wing, and we have never missed a beat. Before Roger came along, I handled the finances in the early stages and managed to get through, but when Roger came along with his knowledge and experience, we were able to jump to another level. Over the years, Roger has worked miracles, and we would not have made it without him. One major fact can I have experienced is that only financial people should handle finances. Roger and I, at times, had to find ways to pay for programs, and I know I put him through hell, but he never complained. He would always say in his very calm demeanor, "Is this something we need to do?" My answer usually was "Yes," and then we would make it happen. Roger and I have become very close over the years. We share our very private lives with each other, and when I need to talk, I reach out to Roger. Roger has taught me to look at all options before I make a decision. In my darkest time, Roger has been there for my family and me.

Linda Saul was a middle-aged Jewish woman who Roger met in the late '90s. Linda found out about our organization and wanted to dedicate some time. Linda was a grant writer and one of the most committed people that I ever met. Linda spent the last years of her life working with us, and it hurt us badly when she died in 2009. Linda would take public transportation on the coldest day of the year to make it to a R.I.S.E. event. One day, I called Linda and said, "I do not want you to come out today because the weather is so horrible." About five minutes before the event started, I saw Linda come through the door. I just shook my head. Here you have this middle-aged White woman traveling a long distance to assist us, and this is not even her community. Linda was a special person, and we will miss her.

Faye Feller is another White woman who has given so much of herself to the R.I.S.E. program. Faye and I have put together some of the most successful programs that I have ever been a part of for over twenty-five years. Faye's specialty is the environment, and she really knows her stuff. Faye will go into the toughest neighborhood in the city and work with the toughest children. She believes that if you show children you care, they will respond positively. Faye and I have taken children on boats, through forests, mountains, and beaches. Faye's programs were interactive, and the children really loved to participate. Faye and I shared a special relationship until she died, and she is sorely missed. I learned a lot working with Faye; she was extremely committed to people. Faye also introduced us to Heidi and Captain Robert Cook, a great committed couple who have been instrumental in assisting our organization. Working with Faye and others has influenced my views on certain parts of life. Race is never an issue when people really care about each other. I have worked with some very good people of all races over the years, but these two women were really special to us.

Bernard Gassaway is the "Obama" of education. He is the most committed person that I have ever met in my life. Bernard is the chairman of our board, but that is very minor when you consider what he is in the Black community. Bernard is the one person who can fix education in America. Bernard is someone who went through a lot as a child, and through his experiences, he can relate to many of the children. Gass, as we affectionally call him, came from a rough childhood like me and was raised by his mother. Gass was the principal of Boys & Girls High School, one of the toughest schools in America. He has worked as a principal in several schools in New York City and was the senior superintendent of Alternative Schools in the late '90s. When you spend time with Gass around children, you see and feel his need to create positive change. Gass is someone who really understands what needs to be done as it relates to education and our children. Gass is a successful author, and all educators and parents should read his books. His views on transforming education into a child first system are special and lead a clear path to successful communities. He will never sell our children out and stand up to what is right without hesitation. Gass, Roger, and I have put together some fantastic programs over the years, and we have done the work of a huge corporation. We were a perfect team and continue to be that today. We have slowed down, but a lot is being accomplished behind the scenes.

Jermaine Miller is a special person to my family, the R.I.S.E. organization and me. Jermaine was a young man who was part of our program since he was a young child. If I were selecting a prototype child for any inner-city program, it would be Jermaine Miller. Jermaine was a young man who was an example of a student-athlete who went on to graduate college, develop into a man, marry his high school sweetheart, select the perfect profession, have and raise his children, and then come back to the community and serve the people free of charge. Jermaine and I were close, and he spent a great deal of time with me in his younger days. Jermaine's entire life revolved around him working with children where he was deeply committed. There are not a lot of people like us that chose to dedicate our time to the community free of charge. The new model of today is that people who work with children charge a fee for their services. That is not my way, nor was it his. I will not judge and have learned to accept what others do because the world changes. I was honored to have Jermaine and his brother-in-law, Larry Cave, take over the day-to-day operations of R.I.S.E. through their CGE LAB program. R.I.S.E. has sponsored many organizations over the years, providing start-up funds, operating funds, training, mentoring, administrative assistance, proposal writing, staffing, and support. Jermaine and Larry were focused and were doing an excellent job in the community. I am really proud of Jermaine and Larry and conflicted about what I should do at this point. Larry will continue to provide services. We have already had that conversation, and I have great confidence in his ability to continue to provide leadership. I, on the other hand, feel the need to get back in the community in honor of Jermaine and do more, but I do not want to get in the way. At sixty years old, I can do more standing back and providing direction rather than jumping in. I hope I will find the balance soon because losing Jermaine really hurt me personally and the community as well. It was a wake-up call for many in the community when the COVID-19 touched us in real-time. We will honor Jermaine when the time is right. He deserves it. I miss you, Maine. You were special. I love you!

Richard Sha Anderson is another committed person that gave much of his time to the organization. He was a New York City detective but never pulled that card in the hood. He spent time with known criminals but treated them with respect, and they respected him as well. He worked with many of the youth and ran the gym for many years. Sha and I have always been close and continue that relationship today. He also is one of the best shooters in New York City High School basketball history.

Corey Jones is also a product of the organization. Corey worked many years with us giving back to the community. He came up through R.I.S.E. and has gone on to be a successful entrepreneur with his lovely wife Delores and their beautiful twins now in college. Corey has always been mature and has been an example for many in the hood and has been there for my family and me without hesitation.

David Reed is another R.I.S.E. product that came through the organization. David was heavy in the streets as a young teen and on the way to either death or prison before we intervened. We assisted David with graduating high school and then employment in the corporate world. David gave me challenges during this time but eventually learned how to cope and in between gaining real-life working experience matured as a man. Today, David is an administrator at a well- respected hospital while also operating his own print shop. He is a testimonial to what our program stands for.

R.I.S.E. has been in existence for thirty-seven years, and in that time, we have serviced thousands of participants free of charge. While many organizations like to talk about their accomplishments, we seldom do. We are a grassroots organization with a CBO mask that we pull out when needed. We stay connected to the community and have accomplished more than anybody during our tenure. Few have done the work we have done and impacted as many people as we have. People try to put us in a box as a recreational organization, and we laugh because we are a movement with a mission of uplifting people and families. Recreation was our enticement to get people involved, and it has always been the best form of that. We understood it early and utilized it to our advantage. Our model has been and still is utilized by many organizations today. From our famous bus rides to our NYC tough as nails gym life. From our park clean-ups to our mortgage assistance programs, we have done it all and will continue until we can't. I have traveled all over in my life, and it is not uncommon for me to come in contact with a former R.I.S.E. participant. I hear a voice that says, "Yo, G," and the next thing, I see a familiar face and smile. Usually, I can remember the name, but I always remember the face.

In the late '90s, we took about fifty young men on a camping trip during Memorial Day weekend. During this trip, these young men would be exposed to the outdoors in a way that they never anticipated. They would see a huge grizzly bear, walk through the mountains in the pitch darkness where you had to hold hands or be lost, be assigned chores, and have a weekend full of fun. One night on the trip, the campers went too far, playing around, and I decided to see where it would go. I let them think it was a done deal. About five o'clock in the morning, I made them all get up and go outside in the chilly morning air and form lines of ten across. By this time, it started to rain, and I made them take their shirts off and perform calisthenics for about forty-five minutes. Every one of these young men did exactly what they were told without much resistance. They understood they were wrong and accepted the punishment. After that, we played ball and then had one of the greatest breakfasts, including pancakes, bacon, eggs, grits, and fruit. What many fail to understand is that young people are crying out for discipline and love. The problem is many adults do not know how to show love and implement discipline. We have never had a problem in these areas. Many from this group have gone on to do great things and always mention this event as a defining time in their lives. Gass and I have become very close over the years, and when we both had some tough times, we counted on each other for support. I strongly believe that the president should put Gass in charge of education if he really wants to see change. He is more qualified than anyone, and most of all, he really cares. I would do anything for Gass, Rog, and some of the others who have supported our mission at R.I.S.E. We were a special group of people that the powers would never allow to get too much funding. They knew if we did, we could build a model for other organizations to follow and keep our people out of prisons. I will die an advocate for children and their rights, it is important to me. If it is not important to you now, I hope when you finish reading my work it will be then.

Part Two

Auntie and Uncle Walley

My aunt Louise Walley was a special person. Other than my mother as my primary caretaker, she was the most important person to me in my life. My brother and I called her Auntie, and she was everything the name was meant to be. She was the person that made everything all right, no matter what the situation was. Don't get it twisted; she would spoil us to death but would not hesitate to put her foot in our ass if need be. The other great thing about her was that she also kept my mother strong and on track. Being a single mother is tough and having my aunt around made things easier for my mother. Auntie was a pretty woman with hair down to her waist. She wore the best clothes and drove the best cars as well. Her husband, Uncle Wally, owned and operated his own Esso (Exxon) gas station. He was a great businessman and owned this business and several others. The irony, however, was that he died a poor man many years later after taking care of so many people. That is the story of so many Black families. My mother worked for my uncle and handled the finances for the gas station and his other businesses. Having my mother at the gas station worked out well for my Uncle; many men would bring their cars for service just to flirt with my mother. My uncle was very well respected, and it was well deserved because it was rare for a Black man to have a business of this stature in the '60s. My Uncle and Aunt lived a big beautiful house in St. Albans, Queens. The house had beautiful furniture, and my Aunt was an excellent housekeeper. She was not the type to have a maid; she wanted to do her own work and boy did she. The house was always spotless, and everything stayed in its place. My aunt was very talented, including being an excellent cook, seamstress, housekeeper, and did a lot for her church. Not to compare but I guess in some ways my wife is a lot like my Aunt, and sub-consciously this may be part of the reason she became my wife. There were other factors but like my Aunt, my wife has long hair and her complexion is also light. When I speak of my Aunt people think I am making her out to be an angel and in some ways to a young boy like me she was. I remember my ninth birthday and I wanted some football equipment and it was probably a little expensive for my mother at the time being a single mother, but sure enough Auntie walked through the door with the equipment and I was so excited. As I write this, I am holding back the tears because I can remember this day clearly as ever. There was also the time when one of the upstate New York basketball programs held try-outs for their traveling teams. The try-outs were far away, and we traveled for almost two hours to get there. When we got there, we were among a few Black people in the gym and Auntie was the only woman there. After going through the drills and scrimmages, it was clear that the other Black kids and I were the better players. The coach called all of the kids together to announce who had made the team and to our surprise none of the Black kids had made it. Auntie approached the coach and asked him why none of the Black kids were picked for the team, and the Coach brushed her off. That was a big mistake; Auntie grabbed him by the arm and began cursing him out. The man was shocked and attempted to apologize, but it was too late. My aunt told me to get dressed and we left. The man followed us out to the parking lot, but Auntie wasn't going to listen to anything he said. That day Auntie had on a powder blue suit with a matching hat and white gloves (she always wore white gloves) and when we got into the car that really shocked him because we were driving the powder blue Fleetwood Cadillac. His jaw dropped as we pulled away. On the way back, Auntie told me how I would always be faced with obstacles and never let anyone treat you like shit. We stopped at a diner and ate and had ice cream; after that it really didn't matter to me that what had happened. I was proud of Auntie and every time I think of that day, I fight a little harder for some of the kids I care about.

I have always had great respect for women; this was something that was instilled in me as a little boy. This is something that is missing today. Young women and particularly young boys need to be educated on the importance of women in the world, and how they should be treated. It is not enough to expect them to know that violence against women is one of the worst crimes you can commit. It is not enough to expect them to protect all women and treat them as equals. This was part of my educational process from my mother and Auntie. My mother, Auntie, and others have taught me that you fight for things that you believe in, and I will take that to my grave. That day and many others I saw strong women who would not let anyone and particularly men push them around. While I am sympathetic to women that go through challenging times at work and at home, there are times you need to do what you have to do and pick up the pieces later. My children have been taught by their mother and me to respect people, but if someone goes too far, then you need to protect yourself. I have seen a few men in my lifetime get a frying pan upside their heads. I am not advocating domestic violence but!

When I was eleven years old, the worst thing that could happen happened. Auntie was diagnosed with cancer and my family, especially my mother and my Uncle, would never be the same. During the early months of the disease, I would spend a great deal of time by Auntie's bedside reading the Bible to her and watching TV. It was the first time in my life that I ever really read the Bible. Auntie had purchased a pocket size Bible for me and till this day I still have it. As the cancer progressed, Auntie was moved from home to the hospital, and I saw less and less of her. Auntie died soon after that and the funeral was held in Georgia and my brother and I did not attend. My mother did her best preparing us for Auntie's death. My brother and I just blocked it out and tried to move on. We rarely talked about it after that and some might say that we needed therapy, but that just didn't happen in the early '70s. Looking back now, this was a turning point in our lives. For my mother, she was losing the most important person in her life. Auntie was almost twenty years older than my mother and their relationship was much more than as big and little sister. Auntie provided direction and support for my mother and after her death my mother was never the same. While my mother always portrayed confidence and strength and, in some ways, became more independent, she never really trusted anyone like she did Auntie. Auntie understood my mother and while my mother did not need approval from her; she gave her the support she needed as a single mother raising her children in New York City. For my brother and me, not having Auntie in our lives really made us care less about family. We no longer wanted to participate in family functions, and my mother never really forced us to. While my mother kept in contact with the family, we all started to pull away and do our own thing. While we always attended school, our free time was sports and the streets. Years later, I really understood how much one person's death can affect a family. I often wonder what my life would have been like if Auntie was still around. Maybe I would have a normal life and been like some of the nerds that I went to high school with? I have never told anyone this, but there have been times as a grown man when I would think of Auntie and cry. There have also been times when thinking of her kept me from going too far. I love you Louise; I am sorry; I meant Auntie.

DMC

Daisy Mae Clifton is my mother, and throughout her life she has been known as someone you can count on no matter what. I guess this is a quality that I inherited from her because people have always said the same about me. My mother is the youngest daughter and the eighth child of a family of nine children. There is a big gap in the ages of the children with the oldest child (Auntie) almost twenty years older than her. My mother was raised in Florida with some of her nieces and nephews while her family of older brothers and sisters remained in Georgia with her parents. I have heard different tidbits about why this occurred but to be honest I never pursued it or really cared. However, I do know that my mother was not close to her mother, and there was always tension when they were around each other. During this time, many families broke up their large families for a variety of reasons. For my mother, I believe that in some ways it worked out for her being raised by her Aunt and Uncle. My mother had a pretty good childhood under the direction of her Aunt and Uncle and was very popular in the town where they lived. My mother was very attractive, pretty, tall, very fair skinned, and could wear her hair very long or have it cut and wear it in almost any style. Her nails were always long and well kept on both her hands and feet, and she stayed in fashion with stylish clothes and shoes. When I was young, I can remember men always trying to flirt with my mother. She would always handle it well. One day while my brother and I were at my mothers job, an older man entered; my mother was dancing (mostly shaking her hips) and the man said to her, "Hey baby why don't you cut your motor baby and let me run it for you" ; my brother and I laughed and my mother smiled and said no thank you. This is what many children experience when you have a single mother. Men really never care about the children. Their interest is purely selfish, and mothers must be super alert to a man's intentions. My mother never remarried, and she made it clear she had no intention of doing so. Her young marriage to my father from what I understood was always rocky. However, one thing my mother never did was talk negative about my father to my brother and me. My mother let me, and my brother know that she was never going to force a

61

man on us. Going through life my brother and I really appreciated this. While my mother did have relationships with men, we never called anyone "Daddy" and she never let them get too close to us. Today many young mothers need to follow this example of not mixing foreign men with their children. Too many enter into relationships with men that go bad, and they have fully exposed these men to their children. When you have children, your life does not fully belong to you. It is not fair, but that is your reality. Take it from someone who grew up living in that world. You must be very careful of the people you expose your children to. You cannot turn it on and off like a faucet.

One day I remember coming home from school; and finding my mother and a couple of family members huddled in my living room. One of my cousins had had a major altercation with her husband who was known for beating her. This time, however, he went too far, and she had taken a knife and defended herself with the results being fatal. My mother told everyone to remain at our house while she went alone to my cousin's house where everything had taken place. About two hours later my mother returned with my cousin and everyone then went back to the house and the police were called. My cousin was arrested but did not spend much time in jail. The case was eventually dismissed. Later my mother sat my brother and me down and explained some of it to us and said in her very confident tone that sometimes you have "to do what you gotta do." In times of emergency, my mother was usually the person my family reached out to. I was proud that my mother was a person who got results, and today I have become that person. Another incident I recall was when one of my minor female cousins became pregnant by her teacher. My mother and other family called a meeting with the teacher. The man was under some heated pressure during the meeting and things got out of hand. I remember hearing a lot of noise then my mother and a couple of her female family members whipped that man's ass. He left that house that night agreeing to meet all of their requests.

As my brother and I got older, we were given more and more freedom. While some may differ with this way to raise your children it worked for us. We always went to school and stayed away from major trouble and sports were a big factor in both of our lives. However, we also managed to find ourselves in the thick of things one way or another. My brother had his friends, and I had mine and then there were those that we shared. For the most part our home was open to our friends, and they all would love to come to our house because we usually had the house to ourselves. My mother had certain rules, including keeping the house neat and always washing your dishes and keeping the kitchen tight. My friends respected these rules, and it wasn't rare to see one of them wash dishes and cooking in our apartment. Going through high school, my brother and I lived more like college students. We both went to school and either worked or hustled to keep money in our pockets. This was fine with us because we were raised to be responsible. We had keys at an early age and never lost them the way kids do now.

Later in my mother's life she was involved in a serious accident and developed some health issues. She maintained her mind but never really moved around they way she did before. I like the way my mother raised us; it gave us real life experience, which has really made me strong for my entire life. I never had a relationship with my father, grandparents (both sides) and most of my other extended family. Growing up in New York City is different; you get caught up in so much, and your friends usually replace your family in some ways. I love my family and would do whatever I could to assist one of them, but I really don't know most of them. I plan to go to a family reunion one year, but usually in the summer when they are held, I have been busy working with children. That has been my passion, and I enjoy it.

My mother is very dear to me, and I am working harder and harder to ensure that I can make the rest of her life enjoyable. Now in her 80's she has good days and bad days. I live with guilt at times because I want to do more for her, but I am limited because I still have to maintain my life as well. There are days I have a battle within myself regarding the time I spend with her because I get pulled away on other projects. It is hard to get her to come out due to the limitations on her legs and her stubbornness regarding using a wheelchair. My children love their grandmother, and I am happy that she has always been in their lives. My wife and my mother have always gotten along, so I never really had the drama that some men are exposed to. My mother lives with my Aunt Ruth who is also in her 80's. We call them the "Golden Girls," and together they comprise all four characters of the sitcom. They battle of attention; they argue occasionally, but the situation is perfect for them both. I really dread the day when the situation changes whatever that means. Let me move on.

My childhood friend Billy (more like a brother) has been instrumental in taking care of my mother and my aunt. In fact, they call him before me in most cases. In their minds, they believe they are bothering me or interrupting my day to ask me for assistance. Between Billy and I, we manage to do a pretty good job of keeping them going. I do not know what I would do without Billy. If you know Billy, then you know.

I would not call my mother the traditional mother by any means. The way she raised my brother and me to be responsible I believe works out well when you are honest with your children. My mother was always honest with us and for the most part we were honest with her. This meant at times being silent because you had the situation under control, and there was no reason to tell her anything. My mother was connected to the streets and may not have known everything, but she knew the jest of the situation. She trusted us to make the right decisions and for the most part we did. Too many men are still under their mother's wings long after they have passed adulthood. I am not saying that after a certain age you are a man, but some of these guys are ridiculous. My mother spent a lot of time with my brother and me when we were young. We consistently went to the movies, plays, circuses, trips, and especially to eat out. I have followed this model with my children, and they are doing the same. Those years when I needed my mother the most, the early years, she was there, and I will always love and appreciate that.

When I became a teenager, I got my first job and became involved in various ways of earning money. I never had to ask my mother for money and in some ways, it prepared me for adulthood at a young age. If you asked me what I wanted to be as a little boy my answer would be grown, so I could do what I wanted. I appreciate the way my mother raised me. I think with the COVID-19 pandemic more parents are going to have to learn to trust their children to take care of themselves at younger ages. Being a single parent is tough, and I made a vow to myself that I would always be there for my children and I have. My mother set a strong foundation for us, and besides being a strong, independent woman, she is a hell of a gambler. By the way, I need to tell her about a dream I had last night so she can pick some numbers.

Father's Day

Father's Day is a strange day for me. As an adult, it has been great because my family has always made me feel special. They always buy me nice things, and we always go out and eat. I have a great family, and we spend quality time together. In my early years with my wife, I would usually spend time with her family, which gave me an idea of how special these days were. As a child I always blocked it out. I wonder how many children block this day out today. I cannot remember any previous Father's Day's as a child. I remember many Mother's Days, including my brother and I going to the local drug store and purchasing Jean Nate perfume sets to give to my mother. Contact with my father did not exist, and to be honest my brother and I really didn't care. At a young age, we were immune to missing my father or any other man. While some may look at this as sad, it is the reality for many children particularly in the Black community. When Father's Day was enacted, I wonder if anyone thought about the psychological effect it would have on the Black community. So many children do not have fathers in their lives in the hood. What are they supposed to do for the day? Are they supposed to smile and act like they really don't care? Should they pretend someone else is their father who is not? For my brother and I, we just never talked about it, and it went away just like many of the men who were part of our lives in one way or another. Men came and men went. Some were coaches and teachers, others were mother's boyfriends on the block, and one thing they shared in common was that they would not be around for long.

In the hood mothers would tell their kids that their boyfriends were their uncles. This would backfire every time because at times kids can be cruel, and it wasn't unusual for one of them to hear that their mother was screwing their uncle. Some even called these men uncle even though they slept in the room with their mother.

In the Black community, we have done a horrible job as men of consistently raising our children as fathers. In some cases, we know that there has been an organized agenda to ensure that men are separated from their families. However, we must overcome this and fight to be in our children's lives. It is easy to stay away. Some of you really think that paying child support is enough; well it is not. Your children need you in their everyday lives. My greatest accomplishment in life has come as a father. I never had one, so this is really special to me. Being a father has been on the job training for me; I have made some mistakes, but there is nothing that I can compare it to. I have become a pretty good grandfather at this point, and I am so excited when I get to spend time with my grandkids. I have six grandkids: Heaven, Taelyn, Lil Gary, Harper and Tyler (twins) and Lil Vic. Sometimes we need to have goals that matter and are not attached to money; one of my biggest goals is being the best grandfather I can be. This is one for me. My grandkids are precious to me. They have changed my life in some ways. They give me motivation and strength. I got to spend a lot of time with my grandchildren before the COVID-19 pandemic. That has changed at least temporarily, and it has taught me not to take things for granted. My wife and I both planned years ago that we would be available for our grandkids when the time came, and both left the corporate world early to set our lives up for this. It has been a challenge in some ways for us but having the autonomy to plan our daily schedules has been priceless. We have been available for our children and grandchildren in some instances where it would have been extremely difficult.

Again, this is an area that is foreign to me because I never spent time with grandparents. I am not angry or upset for not having a father or grandparents in my life. The words Grandma, Grandpa, Nana, Daddy, Dad, are words I never used. No one is to blame; it just fell that way. I hope others will read this and understand how important family is, especially as you get older. Value everyday you spend on this earth and can be there for your family. Males who do not take care of their children are not MEN! I do not think anyone wants to argue the point.

In the early 2000's many states and cities have implemented "Fatherhood Programs," trying to focus on the absence of fathers in poorer communities. In many cases, the sponsoring agencies were trying to compile information on fathers to collect child support and had a very narrow scope of actually assisting the child or the father. When they would approach us, we would brush them off quickly, and after a while, they got the message. Be careful who you share your data with; many of these CBO's and governmental agencies are worst than the desperate people in the streets. They will do whatever it takes to serve their bosses.

While setting up these fatherhood programs, may have been a small step in the right direction, we also need to look at changing how employers view ex-convicts. It is a major contradiction to label incarceration rehabilitation when you are never given a chance upon your release. Many of these ex-convicts want to prove themselves and begin to be part of their children's lives but society (they) really doesn't want this; they want you to return to prison so they can continue to make money. While spending time is more important than financial support when dealing with children, after a while you really need some money for the relationship to grow. Fathers have to have financial resources in order for them to build a relationship with a child. If you do not have money sooner or later the child will start to move away from you. This is a reality that many men face, and in some cases, they have brought it upon themselves. You have to overcome these odds fathers. It won't be easy, but you have to find a way.

At R.I.S.E., we pride ourselves in having an excellent Fathering Program, which we have operated since 1990. Every Sunday morning you can find us at our site providing recreation, mentoring, and counseling for men young and old of the community. We provide guidance for young fathers, provide counseling for those involved in domestic violence and other drama; we prepare people for court, provide necessary documentation for employment, notarize documents free of charge, chastise those who have crossed the line, but most of all we show love to men in the community that need it. We have received awards for our work, but the biggest reward for us is that we see men who were confused become good fathers. When fathers and sons interact, they build strong relationships. We have had many men who raised their children through our program a fact that we are extremely proud of.

Every year on Father's Day we have a huge cook out where we feed the fathers and many in the community. I have developed some great relationships over the years with many of the brothers in the community. Lil, Serg, Groovy, Sha, BJ, Rah, Red Rum, the Carter brothers (True and BJ) and many others share a special place at R.I.S.E. and the community. Many of them have assisted us with developing young fathers. Their influence and sharing their personal lives with young men has been instrumental in these young men's development. We all share a special bond that has grown year by year. This year we were unable to host our annual cookout due to the pandemic, but Serg not letting you off the hook my brother; we will make up for it next year. Love you'll.

Society needs a major overhaul of its judicial system, as it pertains to fathers. Employers must begin to accept ex-felons who have done their time and have developed skills so that they can function in society. Black men must stop making excuses and find a way to be in their children's lives providing love, money, and trust, on a consistent basis. If not, a lot more kids will try and block out Father's Day.

Role Models

Most of the role models in my life have been women: My mother, Auntie, Mrs. Deale and some others. Another woman that stands out to me was my grade school principal Elaine Davis. Ms. Davis was a pretty Black woman who resembled Diane Carroll in some ways. She was an excellent dresser and drove a red convertible. Ms. Davis's office was always neat, and she was always smiling. I loved being a monitor for her, and whatever the task was, I would complete it accurately and quickly. Ms. Davis also had the school under control, and both teachers and students gave her the up most respect. Ms. Davis was a Black principal in the late sixties and early seventies when this was rare. The way she carried herself with class and dignity still stands firm in my mind. Like Mrs. Deale, there have not been many educators and very few that left a positive impression on me.

Many of my best friends' mothers also had a lasting impression on me, including Doris Crutch, Jean Wright, Naomi Hughley, Norma Lilly, Francis Cooper, Chris Spaulding, Juanita Blake-Prather, Marie Davis, Betty Davis, Valerie Reed, and some others. All of these women were strong mothers that understood tough love.

While women again played an important role in my life, there were some men that also have formulated my life principles. My Uncle Cooper was a very good man who was a great father to his children. I rarely see them today but would do whatever I could for them without hesitation. He is ninety-five years old and still drives occasionally, good thing he lives in a less populated area in Georgia. Benjamin Crutch Senior is another man who I have a lot of respect and love for. Ben Sr. is the father of Ben Jr. who I consider my little brother. As noted earlier, the Crutch family was there for me at a tough time in my life. Ben Sr. allowed many of us to share his home and treated us like we were his children. Ron Colson was another man that I considered a role model and an excellent businessman. Ron gave me my first real legal job and taught me a lot about being a responsible worker. His work ethic was to be admired and he educated many of us on entrepreneurship.

Some of my coaches also played an important part in my life. Mr. Renny was my baseball coach and was very amusing because he spent more time playing his numbers than coaching us. The one thing that I can say about Mr. Renny was that he was at the field everyday on time. Phil Green was my basketball coach and the man I have the upmost respect for. Phil took no shit from me and would curse me out if he thought that was needed. I can remember at one game that I was taken out and Phil laid into me. I mumbled something but made sure Phil didn't hear me. That is what is different today with many youths; I knew my place and Phil made sure I stayed in it. Phil may not know it but in some ways, he saved my life because he kept me busy, and I needed to be busy coming from my hood. Ken Fiedler was my high school basketball coach. He was an excellent strategist and was always prepared. He coached my brother and me, and we both didn't see eye to eye with him, but we respected his knowledge of the game. My brother and I were different than the other players on the team, in that we were involved in the street and probably were distracted in some ways. Years later I developed a better relationship with Fiedler and we both understood each other better. I went back to my high school and assisted with the team. It made me feel better, and I strongly believe the same for him. In our era most of the high school coaches were White men but that has changed today in some urban areas. Many of these White coaches were out of touch with the kids and coaching high school sports was just another check. They didn't understand that playing high school sports was a route for us to possibly get a scholarship to college, which for many of us was our only ticket out. We needed Black men with us in the gyms and on the fields and in classrooms because they understood us, and we understood them. I get angry when I think of all of the wasted talent over the years that never had the opportunity to be used because many of us were lost and needed guidance and direction from somebody that really understood our plight. Many of the Black men were in the streets or regulated to jobs where they could not get free time, or they were in prison. Even today when we look at both college and professional sports, we see that White men hold the majority of the head coaching positions. This is not an indictment on White men, but quite the opposite; this is a wakeup call for Black men. We must overcome the obstacles and be visible and consistent role models for our children. We cannot rely on other people to be the primary role models for our children. This has failed us miserably. They can be involved, but we as men of color have to be the primary role models for our children.

Many of the role models in my life at young were the men I met in the streets. There was Scottie, Rad, Ronnie, Yap, Jimbo, Rob, Guy, Bat, Fleetwood, and some others. While these men were part of the street culture, they also took an interest in some others and me. They were always teaching, and part of their lesson was trying to teach us to have a better life then they had. Some were men who had spent time in prison and while their lives seemed attractive now, they had played a big price. Most of the street hustlers never glamorized their lives; they were quick to tell us to stay in school and strive for the best in life. When I went away to college and missed the streets, I can remember Yap telling me one day, "Green Eyes, you are smart, and a good ball player; stay your ass in school." Hearing that from him meant far more to me than hearing it from people I didn't know or who were being phony. Even today the street hustlers play an important role in the lives of our youth. Many adults (hypocrites) are quick to degrade them instead of embracing their lives as teaching tools for our youth. I can tell you I learned far more from them than in any classroom. If we expect to create change in our community, we must incorporate everyone into the process. Remember it takes a village to raise a child! Years ago, Charles Barkley made it clear when he said that athletes and entertainers should not be considered "role models." I agreed right away because we are quick to put people on a pedestal simply because they have a special talent. Take away that special talent, and they are just like the rest of us.

Today, if I was looking for people to speak with a group of kids, the pool I would pick from would include NBA and NFL players, Rap Music and R& B artists, actors and actresses of Black related content, and people from the streets. These are the people that urban youth want to hear from. You can fool yourself and bring in people from other industries, but they will be on their phones checking their Instagram. I am very impressed with both the NBA and the Rap music industry. They are the leaders right now in driving Black America and many young people of color. Lebron, Kobe (RIP) before he passed, Melo, Dwayne Wade and some others really showed their leadership skills and their desire to see change for their people. It helps that they are wealthy and have a platform, but if that was the case, they could mind their business and stay above the fray. They have power and have chosen to pull their sleeves up and get in the fight and should be commended for it. The work Jay-Z is doing is extremely important and he and other rappers have also chosen to get in the fight for Black people. Don't let agitators get you to question the motives of people like Jay-Z and others. When Hov was doing whatever he was doing with the NFL, please believe part of his plan was to bring along as many qualified Black people as possible for future deals and positions. The key word here is qualified, and the reason I say that is because we have no room for era when you are dealing with a financial juggernaut like the NFL. Hov has a plan but he can't reveal it to you, so what do you do; you start conversations in the barbershops about he is being selfish and has flipped on the hood. Please stop the bullshit and become better educated on the art of doing business. Stop repeating things that you have no factual data to support. When you see others trying to elevate the race, jump on the bandwagon and assist in the struggle.

I believe the way I have led my life I have been a role model for many. I am no angel, as you can see by now, but I work hard for the many youth that have trusted me over the years. I urge you to do the same.

Sunday Mornings

Since 1990 I have done the same thing every Sunday morning. If anyone wanted to kill me, I would be an easy target. We call it "Church" in the hood and that is what it is to us. At R.I.S.E. we go through great lengths for our fathers to feel special about who they are. Every Sunday we hold our weekly program rain or shine. Our fathers come out to network, work out, and most of all spend time with men who understand their lives. No women are allowed on Sunday mornings, but men are encouraged to bring their children. This is not a slap at anyone; this program was developed for men to work out their problems, and sometimes men need to be separated from the women in their lives and vice versa to think things out. Our program has won several awards over the years, and I have been acknowledged on several occasions. That really doesn't matter to me; it is important to see men feeling good about themselves. When I see Groovy, Daddy, Dullah, CJ, Sha, Gil, Face, Malik, Corey, Aleek, Milk, BJ, Donald, Miguel, Mike B., Mapp, Jermaine, Trysse, Lil, Wheel, Russ, Rha, and especially Red Rum, I know everything is going to be all right. We have about 25-35 men who consistently take part in our Sunday program and each week we also have guests. Everyone one of them gives back to the community in some shape, form, and fashion. Over the years our fathers have grown as men and especially fathers. This year we lost two very special members of our community Jermaine and Dave. Both were men who were giving back to the community in many ways and were role models to many youths.

Our recreation is very competitive, and to be frank is rough, which has discouraged some guests from coming back. We prefer it that way, and have also turned many away because we believed they were a distraction to overall program. We advertise our gym as the "Toughest in the World," and we believe it. Many of the guys are pros, ex-college stars, high school stars, and playground legends. Some of the men are performing well in life; others are down on their luck. Occupations can range from blue-collar worker to corporate manager to street hustler. When you walk in the gym you are part of us, and it matters. Many of the guys have gotten their lives together on Sunday mornings, including finding employment to getting valuable advice on how to handle a relationship. Others have developed their fathering skills while spending time with their children. To play with us, you have to have talent, but most of all you have to have an understanding of the game. Guys go all out on Sunday to win games, including diving for loose balls, fouling extra hard if necessary, and chewing out someone for not hustling. I can remember an occasion when we had a great turnout on Thanksgiving weekend; guys were going extra hard; there was a loose ball and about five to six players went for the ball and for more than a minute, we all fought for the ball, nobody called, nobody wined, we just kept playing. Another time a player who had a reputation came to the gym and thought he was going to dominate our gym. He tried to go to the basket and the guys let him have it. He tried calling and was quickly reminded there are no fouls; the defender must give you the ball as a courtesy. Sometimes you get it sometimes you don't and that is a life lesson we teach. We give the defense the opportunity to be honest. It works! In all the years of the program, we have never had a fight, which is a testimonial to the program. We bring together some of the toughest men in New York City at 8:00 AM (guys are rarely late) and put them in a super competitive environment where the game is as physical as it gets, and they compete and find respect for each other. Over the years, I have heard people criticize our play, but we have helped so many men over the years get their lives together, which is a testimony to the success of the program. This is a model program that should be replicated in many urban communities. It emphasizes some extremely important elements of life, including teamwork, respect, discipline, mentoring, counseling, fathering, love, and most of all understanding. Just remember no fouls!

Child Support

Child support is a "Catch 22" in the hood. It is a necessary tool for the custodial parent to receive financial support from the other parent. However, it has taken on its own life over the years. In theory it works, but it causes so much turmoil you wonder overall how effective it really is? Psychologically you wonder the affect it has on all parties involved. For the mother and father in many cases, they become enemies rather than function as a team. For the children, they become confused pawns caught in the middle. My experience with child support is as a third party. I have never paid child support because my children have always lived with me. I am happy to say this; however, the flip side to this is that I am the product of a single-parent family, so I firmly understand how child support affects one's life. I witnessed firsthand how my mother provided for us without support from my father. In addition, I have operated a very successful fatherhood program for over thirty years, providing services on a consistent basis and working with hundreds of men.

In the majority of cases, the woman is usually the custodial parent and the primary caretaker. Many of the men are disgruntled and believe they never got a fair shake in court. In many cases, they are right. The problem for them is that they are paying the price for all of the men who never took care of their children. It is not fair, and it is bullshit, but moving forward you know when you go to court for a child support hearing, go expecting the worse. I have spent time in court with many fathers who were doing a good job, and they still got screwed. They had no problem in supporting their children. Their issue came with the mother and their relationship, and the inability of both to function as a team. In some of these cases, these men were forced to live in poor conditions because that is all they could afford after paying their child support. This made them very bitter and affected their relationship with their child. On the other hand, the woman deserved the opportunity to move on and not struggle as the custodial parent receiving the financial support on a consistent basis. However, this gets complicated because in many cases they both enter into new relationships and other people get involved and before you know it the child is suffering. This is a common occurrence that pains me a great deal. I grew up in a home where my mother never received child support and never asked. I knew many women that came from this mindset. They were determined to raise their child on their own, and in most cases did an incredible job. Family planning is missing in the Black community. In other cultures, couples develop a solid plan on when they will have children. Birth control is utilized, developing a solid relationship, and building finances is part of the overall plan. In the Black community, many children are the result of teenage pregnancy where both parents are not prepared for the challenge. Raising children is a challenge because you never really know what lies ahead. I never had a father in my life but for me this made me more determined to be in my children's lives. While my mother did a great job, and I never missed my father, I still had no clue what to do when I became a father. Yes, I saw some of my friend's fathers, but it was not something that I consistently saw everyday. Our children need to see consistent models of fatherhood so strong families can be developed. Before children are conceived, both parties should have a firm understanding that they will work together as parents regardless of what happens in their relationship. The courts have decided the fate of too many children and really have no understanding of the Black community. The key is for mature parents to work out a reasonable agreement that puts the child first. Ensuring that the child has everything he or she needs is the priority. Again, I acknowledge historically too many Black men have avoided paying child support, but we need to wipe the slate clean and start from scratch. Black men need to step up to the plate acknowledge their children and develop a solid plan with the mother to insure both financial and emotional support. We cannot move forward as a group until then. DNA testing has added another dilemma to whole child support monster. Some women and men get offended when DNA testing is suggested. This component has added assurance to both parties to who the father is. I had a father from our program that had been paying child support for a couple of years and then decided to have a DNA test. After taking the test, he discovered he was not the father. After the discovery, he informed the courts so that he could be relieved of child support and be reimbursed for the error. The whole process was a nightmare and on top of that he would have to file a civil suit to be compensated. Wouldn't you think that he should have been immediately compensated and then the biological father held accountable? Not so simple, because the woman was not sure who the father was. Well shouldn't she be held accountable? Not so simple either; the case dragged on and on. Eventually, he was relieved of his child support obligations, but the emotional and financial scars remained for all involved. DNA testing should be done before any father signs a birth certificate. This would save a lot of money and time for all involved. More importantly, it would ensure that a child knows who his or her father is. How do children feel when they have grown attached to someone only to find out later that this person is not their father?

The whole system needs to be thrown out and a new system that makes sense implemented. The major steps that really need to be taken do not involve the courts. Men and women who have consensual unprotected sex need to agree that if a child is conceived that both will be responsible for the child until he or she reaches adulthood. We must take the courts out of our lives in the Black community. Courts have never been fair and never will be fair to us; no one can dispute that. Another issue involves fathers that are in prison. When a man is incarcerated, his child support meter continues to run. When he is released, he usually owes thousands of dollars in child support with no job in sight. If he is fortunate enough to find a legal job, then child support will take a significant portion, and he will barely survive. What is he supposed to do? Some of you buppies will be quick to say, "Well then you should have never committed a crime."   My answer to that is please look at law enforcement, clergy, politicians, some other groups, and even yourself and you will see criminals. There may be different brand of crimes but in the end if it quacks like a duck it's a duck. In many cases this man will not find employment, and this will ultimately push him back into a life of crime where he can earn. This is why we must do a better job from the jump of establishing positive relationships, having protected sex, building finances, and most of all become educated on family planning. There is a percentage of the world that does not want to see Black men as responsible fathers. Their goal is to continue to feed the prison system, a lucrative business for the powers that be. Children that have both parents are more likely to succeed, and boys that have fathers in their lives are less likely to go to prison. We cannot blame them; we must blame ourselves, and the best way to beat them is to not let anything stop you from being a responsible father.

Domestic Violence (Keep Your Hands to Yourself)

I have three daughters and one thing that I have instilled in them is that no man should ever put his hands on them. I have also emphasized that they should not put their hands on any man as well. My children were raised in a home where domestic violence was never an issue. This is very important because you have some men that have committed domestic violence and then have issues with other men that have committed it against a member of their family. You must practice what you preach. I strongly believe that domestic violence is a learned behavior. Some men commit this act in front of their children giving them the illusion that this is normal behavior. In the world today the laws have changed, and an act of domestic violence has major affects on the family as a whole. Jobs can be lost, finances reduced, and imprisonment a reality. I have witnessed some acts of domestic violence in my lifetime and have always done my best to diffuse the situation. When I was younger, I can remember an incident with a close friend of mine Hester who was always quick to put his hands-on women. He was really out of control this day, and I tried my best to keep him subdued. After defusing the situation, a couple of times, he went ballistic and began hitting his girlfriend. I jumped in and tried to restrain him only to be accidentally punched in my face. He apologized to me immediately, but the damage was done. While our relationship stayed the same, it really bothered me how quickly he would resort to violence against women. Later in my life, I would see other men lose their temper and hit women. While I fully understand there are other issues that may be involved, women must draw the line with this issue. I have taught my children to never accept this situation from any man. If a man hits, pushes, or worse, you first, then the relationship is over. There is nothing to talk about other than how do we complete the separation. There may come a day when you work it out with him, but that will be a new relationship where you as a woman have laid out some serious ground rules. No matter what the circumstances are a MAN should leave the space wherever the conflict is taking place and there is a chance that violence will occur. That is a universal answer to domestic violence. WOMEN, you have to let him leave. Sometimes that very simple reaction will save a relationship and give both parties time to think. When emotions are running high, mistakes are made. Going for a long drive or walk or calling a close friend to vent will do wonders. You cannot block the door or continue to grab him so he will not leave. In "Dead Presidents" when Larenz Tate (Anthony) tries to leave during a heated argument with Rose Jackson (Juanita) over infidelity, and she attempts so stop him by blocking the door, he ends up choking her. This is an example of things getting out of hand. The best conversations take place when cooler heads prevail.

Alcohol and drugs also play a major role in domestic violence situations. Both men and women act out of character when they are under the influence. I can remember being at a party and a married woman I know who had a few too many was dancing very provocatively with another man (not her husband). Well as time went on, she really went overboard and everyone at the party was shocked. Her husband who had been drinking as well remained calm, but you could see he was getting upset. After a while he jumped up and snatched her by the arm and took her into the back room to talk. We all heard a lot of noise and after a while they emerged from the room and went straight for the door both looking disheveled and embarrassed. This was a case where the consumption of alcohol played a major role in creating a negative incident. As adults we must be mindful of the affects of alcohol and drugs. I am not preaching, but I have seen some very cool customers lose total control under the influence.

When the whole Rihanna and Chris Brown drama came out, I felt for both of the young people. While there were issues of violence, I did not consider this your prototype "domestic violence" issue. While I do not know all of the facts and to be honest it is really nobody's business, it became a lighting rod for some groups. To me this was more the product of poor leadership or to be honest poor parenting. Here you had two beautiful young people with a lot of money, celebrity status, and if accounts are accurate under the influence of alcohol. In an era of Twitter, Facebook, Instagram, and other products of technology trouble is

81

waiting right around the corner, especially when you throw in underage drinking. I do believe Chris was wrong, but I also believe both young people were given too much freedom to function as adults without the experience to navigate through tough relationship issues. I know a lot of people a lot older and if you put them in the same situation things could get worse. I love Rihanna and she deserved better; in some ways she reminds me of my daughters, which means she is no joke when she has her mind set on something. I love Chris as well and he reminds me of the many young men I have mentored over the years that lose their tempers and act out of character. I see Chris growing now; he has been through a lot, and he is proving people wrong. Stay focused Chris you will win. They both need for people to move on from this, and if you do bring it up, you are using the situation to teach about navigating young relationships and nothing else. Young relationships need direction and guidance. When you allow young people to operate as adults, you cannot become angry when mistakes are made. Some of young people are crying out for our interference. This does not mean you need to check their phones, or spy on their Facebook accounts, but you need to have some idea of where they go and who they spend time with. You would be surprised how many young girls are strippers and young men who belong to gangs that their parents have no clue. Again, what we do as adults impacts our children's lives. If domestic violence was never a part of your life as a child, it probably will not be a part of your life as an adult, no matter what music you hear or movies you watch. So, everybody and especially men keep your hands to yourself, and when necessary, don't hesitate to take a walk.

Tru Asia (Ms. Toni)

I met her in summer of 1978 at a block party. The previous week
I had met her sisters, and they were very nice and attractive
young ladies. I had just graduated from high school and was
scheduled to leave for college in the next couple of months. She
was very pretty with very long hair and had a beautiful smile.
Toni came from a two-parent household with a strict mother and
a strong father. The house they lived in was very week kept and
had a ranch fence, well kept lawn, pool, and looked like no other
house in the neighborhood. When people saw the house, they
automatically assumed her family was rich. While they were far
from poor, they were not rich but lived very comfortably. The
Richie's were compared to the Brady Bunch in some circles
because the family was so clean cut. Bernadette, Toni's mother
was a very proud and strong woman who took no shit from
anybody. She was one of the kindest people you would ever
meet. Mom, as I affectionately referred to her was a lot like my
mother. She could be sweet as cherry pie, but when challenged
she had not problem telling you to go to hell while using some
very choice words. One Holiday Season a few days before
Christmas some burglars broke into her patio and stole all of the
Christmas gifts that she had purchased for the grandkids. There
was a lot of money spent on those gifts. She went out the next
day and purchased every gift again. What impressed me the most
was not that she spent the money again, but that she put the effort
into going to every store again? Nobody would have known if
she didn't duplicate the effort, but it mattered to her. Landon,
Toni's father was very calm and low key. He was a great father in
a time when most children didn't have one. Pop and I shared
some great times together, including discussing sports, current
events, and definitely more then a few drinks. Lanny B. as I
would affectionately call him liked to purchase the best cold cuts,
wines, cheeses, cakes, and chocolates. I loved sitting with him for
long periods while he offered me his delicious treats that he had
purchased each Saturday morning. While I have heard some
horror stories about in-laws, I cannot tell you one bad moment
that I shared with mine. We always got along fine, and I loved
them and miss them today. They always treated me like a son and

never as a son in-law. Two of the hardest periods in my life were when they both died, and my family went through hell in a short period of time between their two separate deaths. Mom and Pop were foster parents for over one hundred kids over a span of years. There commitment to children was evidenced when so many of these children as adults showed up at their funerals.

One of the really special foster kids who was also a R.I.S.E. product was Talib (Sheldon). Talib endured much as a kid but went on to graduate from M.I.T. and Boston University and now is doing great things in his life with his wife and beautiful daughter. He is a testimony to hard work and perseverance. He is part of the Richie family and my brother in-law and we care for him and his family dearly.

When Toni and I got our second apartment in our early 20's, we had a very heated argument. While no physical contact took place, a lot of profanity and throwing each other's things went on, immature behavior but not uncommon for a young couple. I left the apartment and went to my friend's house to calm down. I returned later and things were calm again. The next morning, I went to see Mom and Pop and told them about the incident and assured them that I did not put my hands on their daughter. They both looked at me and said, its alright we understand that things happen, and we appreciate your honesty. Later, Toni approached me and asked you told my parents about last night, and I responded yes, I wanted them to know that I would never put my hands on you. Since Toni and I have lived together (30 years), we have never had any issues involving physical contact. Part of that can be contributed to how we both were raised. In my case, I never really had any man in my life to witness domestic violence, and my mother would not let any man hit her and live to talk about it. Toni's father did not hit her mother, so in both cases there was no negative behavior to learn. Toni's siblings include Kim and Ricky. Kim has always been like a sister to me. She is always looking to have fun. Kim has been a single mother for most of her adult life with five children. She has done a great job for the most part with raising her children. Her oldest children the twins Khalid and Kimora were born the same day as me September 23rd, and we have always been close. Khaliq is my other nephew and is a very generous and reminds me of his grandfather at times. I have been around them their whole lives and love them like they were my own. Khalid came to live with us during his high school years when he was going though some issues. He was doing horribly in school but with a lot of family support from everyone got his shit together and graduated on schedule. It was a perfect case of family coming together to do what is best for the child. My brother's daughter Viola also came to live with us when she had some issues in high school. Her mother Regina recognized that her daughter needed a change and Toni and she worked it out. Viola graduated on time as well and has grown into a strong independent woman. Regina has always had a strong relationship with Toni and me. I wish my brother and Regina would have stayed together. I strongly believe it would have been better for both of them. Regina and I have always remained close, and I consider her my sister. Ricky, Toni's brother, is a die-hard sports fan and coach. Rick and I have always been close and have a very good relationship. Rick is like his father in some ways, including being very generous. His wife Dee-Dee is a sweetheart, and they live in another state but stay connected.

Toni came from a family background that became the cornerstone for our family. Being around her family was like a family education for me. I watched her for years in shaping my daughters. Each week she had a firm schedule that she rarely deviated from. I never had to wash my own clothes and delicious meals were always prepared for our family. The girls always had their hair well kept and were well dressed and after making sure this was done, she did the same for herself. Toni always held some sort of managerial position where she usually mentored younger workers. In '90s Toni was the General Manager of the Shark Bar Restaurant in New York City. For a long period, the Shark Bar was the most popular spot for the Black community in New York City and many movie stars, superstar athletes, rich and famous, would wait hours for a table. Toni worked with a woman

named Lisa who was instrumental in giving Toni her start in the
hospitality business. Lisa had a flair for the business and her and
Toni worked well together. Toni would work with other larger
restaurants after this period, but at the Shark Bar is where she
developed her own style. Toni, Lisa, and some others were like
celebrities in the own right with everyone wanting a table. I can
remember one night sitting with Denzel Washington, Steve
Harvey, and Diddy. When every professional sports team came to
town, they made sure they spent a night at the Shark Bar. The
Shark Bar was a special place in its prime, and there were some
nights being there was a story to tell. In 2009, Toni and I opened
Pretty Toni's Café a soul food restaurant on the border of
Queens, New York City and Long Island. It is a beautiful place
and is growing everyday. Working with her on the project, I had
the opportunity to see how much she really knew about the
business. I have been really impressed with her knowledge,
preparation, and especially her work ethic. I pride myself on how
hard I work, but she may be one of the few people that I met that
has me beat. I guess since I have seen her do things effortlessly
for years, I have taken it for granted, but seeing her take her
vision and turn into a reality was special. She is also my boss and
is quick to let me know that. It is a testimonial to our marriage
that we have been able to work together for eleven years and
counting. Toni has slowly become the matriarch of her family.
She is very reliable, and I realize that I made the right choice in
choosing her to become my wife. For you feminist, she chose me
to be her husband, whatever the case, the shit worked. We still
have a good time together and have overcome some obstacles
over the years like most married couples. We have our moments,
but for the most part rarely have long disagreements. I call her
Tru Asia because that was the name she earned in the hood. We
are a mature couple that understands the value of teamwork. She
has supported my non-profit work, especially early in our
marriage when I would spend long hours at the center working to
keep kids out of prison. When I was in the street doing my thing,
she was patient and worked with me until I eventually evolved
into the man I am today. Toni and I have always shown progress
throughout our marriage. When we first lived together, I moved

in with her in a Brooklyn apartment, which was a far cry from what we were both use to. Since that time almost thirty- seven years ago, we now have a nice home where we can spend quality time with our grandchildren. Our children have all met educational goals, created family businesses with us, built their own families, purchased homes and in addition to being intelligent and beautiful women. I attribute most of this to having a mother to emulate. Again, when you have a model, life is easier, not easy but easier. I have been fortunate to have Toni in my life. We still have many challenges to go; I am not worried; I have a partner that is willing to put up the fight. I defined marriage a long time ago; "It is the ability to deal with someone else's shit." I never thought that I would be married when I was younger, but in retrospect, it is one if not the best decisions that I have made. Today, many will say that marriage is not necessary and in some ways they may be correct. Learn everything you can about your partner, and if you have to hide who you really are, then that marriage is not going to work. You will need that person at some point to really know who you are; otherwise, you are fooling yourself.

Toni's Letter to Gary

What a great read!! Loved that you broached many subjects that helped shape you into the man you are today.

We met when we were both 17 years old, Summer of '78, and it has been a whirlwind in a good way. Forty-Two years have come and gone, and I can honestly say that life has been better for me with you in it. We created and nurtured a loving family that will continue our legacy. Your work ethic, consistency, generosity, integrity and sense of community were the best, hands down that I've witnessed. You have been and continue to be a pillar of the community. You have been the backbone of our family, and I am so very thankful that I got/get to do this life with you.

Thank you for working hard everyday so that we can fulfill our dreams. Thank you for believing in me and supporting me even when it felt like the world was against me. Thank you for giving me enough memories to last a lifetime. Thank you for loving me. Thank you for the absolute privilege and honor of being able to call you my husband and best friend. I'm lucky to have you by my side. I just want you to know how much I appreciate, love you and also how proud I am of you G-Money.

Real Man
Real Dad
Real Talk
Real Nigga

Yeah!!!! That about sums it up!!

Reflections from My Daughters

Temiko

I read your book and I feel it was a great read. All of the chapters gave me an in-debt perspective of your experiences, which impacted you and made you who you are today.

When reading your book, some things were brought to my attention... Somethings I knew and other things I didn't. I always knew about Auntie and your relationship, how you looked up to her and how she was a main person that helped define your character. Your relationship with her was very comparative to Nanna. For me, I have never been the same since her death. I feel a part of me died with Poppa and especially Nanna because it was such a shock and unreal. Since I had Taelyn, many things such as life have been put into perspective. Everything has to be done in advance.... Such as bottles, cooking, cleaning, shopping, etc. My "list" is beneficial and needed everyday.

I remember growing up and always knowing the significance of family and its importance. I always had a day to day schedule. At 5am, I remember hearing the water running in the morning and the front door locking. That would be Daddy! I would then smell chicken or cinnamon toast being made. Dinner, lunch and breakfast was prepared and ready for us. After school, my sisters and I would walk to Nanna's house. She would always say, "3:30-5:30 is homework time." We would rush and get it done so we could watch TV. Daddy would pick us up and take us either home or to the gym. "Wait" we would say because he would walk so fast. Most of the time I would have to run just to keep up. I loved when we would go to Daddy's job for " Take your Daughters to Work Day."

Every Saturday we would go the library and get books and videos. We always knew our Black heritage and its importance. We would have to watch "Eyes on the Prize" on PBS or videos. We also enjoyed going to his "Teenage Pregnancy

Prevention Program." We learned about AIDS and HIV Awareness and created a bond with other young girls in the community.

Daddy always was fresh and clean! Especially when he went to work. He always wore a full suit; shoes were polished, and everything was tailored and crisp. When he would go to work in NYC, it made me want to be there as well. I went to high school not too far from his job. I remember when I turned 16 years old; I got my first Louis Vuitton purse with the matching wallet. Also, inside the wallet there was my very own American Express Gold Card and some other store cards as well. That taught me how to manage money, and pay my bills on time. It still stuck with me till this day. I always want to do better, be the best and set an example for my sisters. I wanted to go to an HSBU, "Howard University," purchase a home, be there for family, start my own business, and have a great husband that would be a great daddy.

Daddy taught me the true meaning of what a father is and what he should be. He should have a tell it like it is mentality, be a great listener, a mentor, be there for you 100% of the time and sometimes piss you off. A man who conceives a child does not mean you are a father. I feel many men today are just sperm donors! Daddy thank you for making me what I am today, and I love you so much for that! Love Miko

Tonita

When I sit back and reflect on each of the moments I have with my Dad, G, whether they are overjoyed, raged, dismal, exciting, I can only ponder one thing in my head...A REAL Man! Now I'm not only saying this because he is my Father, I'm saying this because I truly believe it myself. During my teenage and early adulthood, I've seen a lot; I learned a lot, and I have also gained a lot. I'm going to start with what I learned, because my father, G played a significant role in my learning/education. I can remember as far as when I learned how to read and write, which if I remember correctly as early as 1st grade, my father would

90

give me research papers to write. The funny thing about it is, I wasn't unenthusiastic about completing them. I enjoyed learning about the men and women whom my dad had pictures of displayed in our apartment. It seemed as if W.E.B. Dubois, Harriet Tubman, and Kwame Nkrumah were all a part our family because I saw them every day on my living room wall. My Father taught me about my past.

From all the many things I learned in life, I could definitely say that most of it came from home. Of course, I learned significant information in school as well, but many of the things I did learn The DOE (Department of Education) was not responsible for. Growing up, my mom was the mathematician, and dad was the Editor. When it was time to complete homework, if we didn't understand something, then we knew who to call on. I remember countless times when I thought I completed an assignment, which I knew I rushed through; dad would put a big X right through it. What is this? Do It Over! After a while, I knew I couldn't just hand in nonsense, no matter what it was. That's why I'm such a creative freak when it comes to work and presentations now. All of my work has to stand out now.

My father had this name for me, which was "the rebel without a cause." I laugh at it now because I learned the correct meaning of that phrase as I matured. Growing up, I was always into something. I constantly had my parents worrying about me; I was a confused soul. He never gave up on me and always displayed confidence in me. He told it how it is, meaning how life is. He held my hand but would let go at times so I could make my own decisions. One of the things that my dad used to say to my sisters and me was that he would not tolerate two of the following: 1) His daughters being Drunks, and 2) His daughters selling their pussy. This is still in my head from when I was about 12 years old.

Another one of the most important lessons my father drilled into my head was one on work ethic. He had this saying that he said to my sisters and me at least once a day. "Lazy today, Homeless tomorrow" were his exact words. When I think of this, I remember the early mornings lying in my top bunk at approximately 5:50a.m. The apartment door slams, and I jump out my bed to look out the window and watch my dad walk to the Long Island Railroad. I would look out the window until I actually see the train zoom by which was probably around 6:02a.m. The hilarious thing about it is I used to actually look so hard into the train windows imagining that I see him waving at me. The point of this is that I know my dad was expected to be to work at 9:00am, but instead he arrived to work daily at 7:15a.m. That says a lot about a person.

One thing I remember about my dad and his job in corporate America is that he was like the only Black man with an actual office and not a cubical. I used to walk in his office and see the big-framed pictures of the slave trade and the struggles of our people. I used to think in my head sometimes, did the white people at his job think he was racist? As soon as the thought left my head, a white co-worker would come into the office so excited to speak with my dad. I guess not! My father has accomplished so much, and seeing him do so, makes me want to follow his path. Real Talk!

Living in a community, where as a family we were heavily involved, was hard because majority of the people around you knew who you were. I had to deal with… I'mma tell your pops, or hey your dad knows you out here? That kept me on point at times because I knew my dad would find out whatever it was I was doing that I wasn't supposed to be doing. We are a well-known family. It was a good thing because I had the chance to give back to my community at such a young age. I remember cleaning up parks, working on posters, doing the scoreboard, or keeping records in the scorebook for the ongoing basketball tournaments my dad set up through his organization called R.I.S.E. The R.I.S.E. organization has been there for so many people and that was a great thing for me to see. Being able to be there for someone, to listen, to guide, to teach, and to not give up was what it displayed and still displays to this day. One of the most important lessons that someone can teach a person is to know how to be there for another person.

As I grew older and more mature, my father would tell me some things…some REAL things that took me some time to understand. He told me about his past, and how he chose to live his life. A lot of parents are either afraid or just in denial. I'm glad I knew things about my father that many people hadn't known: the good things, the great things, and the not so good things. It feels good that I won't be reading his book and just learning a whole new side of my father. I know from years and years of engaging in conversation with my dad, watching him, helping him, and being around him that this is Real, and He is my man, my nigga, my DAD!

Toi

Everyone has a father, but everyone may never have a daddy! They say anyone can be a father, but it takes a real man to be a daddy. I was lucky enough to have both a father and daddy in mine. A daddy is supposed to protect you or at least make you feel protected, provide, guide, and nurture you. It's the little things I remember from my childhood that I will cherish always. My dad used to chase us around the house as "The Rhino" where he would nudge us with his head screaming, "No One Can Stop The Rhino"; if you've seen the movie "Liar Liar" starring Jim Carrey, "The Claw" is a good example of how it was. I remember sitting in my living room just listening to old music like Marvin Gaye, The Jackson Five, and Al Green to name a few and looking through the Motown book on top of our coffee table with him. He always made us feel special, not giving my sisters or myself preferential treatment over the next. He went as far as to buy all of us presents on each of our birthday so we wouldn't feel left out. He made my sisters, cousins and myself do book reports on famous influential Black historical figures just so we would know our history, culture, and where we came from. I admired him so much that I got in trouble in elementary school once because I would not stand up for the pledge of allegiance or the school song because he didn't. A couple of my classmates followed suit, and I was sent to the principal's office. He came to my various basketball games and even gave me pointers on my game. He came to my talent shows cheering me on. I could hear him in the front row with my mom. He didn't tolerate my sisters and I fighting. He always would say, "My brother and I never fought; sisters are not supposed to fight." I remember he took me to Miami for my 13th birthday. He asked me did I want a party or to go to Miami, like that was even a competition! It was just me and him; we ate out at restaurants and walked on the strip. I'll never forget that trip! We lived on the 7th floor in Rochdale Village and when my sisters and I would goof off and make a mess in the house, we always knew to hurry up and clean before he came home between 6:00-6:15 p.m. His famous quote was, "Lazy Today, Homeless Tomorrow," and he took great pride in exemplifying and living up to it. He had this distinctive walk that my sisters and I would spot from our terrace all the way from the path, and we would scramble to have things back in order. This wasn't too much of a problem for myself; I've always been the neatest out of my sisters and me. That's a trait I inherited from him. We both are anal retentive and can't sleep until things are in order. I remember once he kicked us out the apartment for two hours because we didn't clean the kitchen. He also had this distinctive mad face where his nostrils flared up and if you got that look you knew you were in trouble. At the dinner table if you didn't finish your food or playing around, he'd look up; bang on the table twice with his fist; point to you and say, "Eat"; then finish his own plate. My dad was and still is the calmer of my parents, and I guess that balances them out. I couldn't ask for better parents. My mother is a strong Black woman that aspires me in ways she'll never know, and my dad does the same. What he's done for the community out of the kindness and genuine well being for our people, especially the youth, is commendable. He's been such a father figure to so many young men who come to him with problems from unemployment, girlfriend issues, street life, child support, and many other issues troubling and crippling our community. I'm just the lucky one who gets to call him Daddy!

Mrs. Deale

My mother Daisy Mae Clifton aka DMC in the late '70s

Five of my six grandkids and me, including Heaven, Taelyn, Little Gary, and the Twins Tyler and Harper

My wife for thirty-five years
Pretty Toni (aka Tru Asia)

My three beautiful daughters on a
family vacation in Las Vegas

Gass and Me at MS 72

Bus ride to upstate New York in late '70s that we sponsored. Hosted my own bus. True in shades with some other street legends

Preme and I at my house in the late '90s for a birthday celebration

Pretty Toni's Cafe

R.I.S.E. Tree

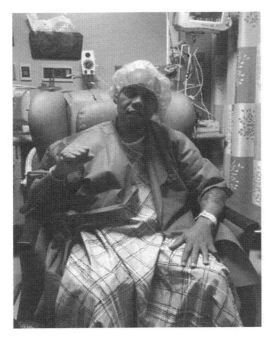

Preparing to go into operating room for my cancer surgery.
Portraying confidence but really nervous

Part Three – Real Talk

Social Studies

In the early years of my schooling, I was always intrigued by "Social Studies." It was the subject that was my favorite in grade school. We learned about America from its evolution and up to the modern day. It was funny being Black and hearing so much about how great America was. The majority of the year we would be introduced to great Americans and their contributions to society. All of these Americans were White, and the curriculum dictated that they only talk about the good things that they contributed to America. It was funny as you got older and had the opportunity to do your own research that you discovered that many of them were power hungry slave owners that had committed some of the most violent crimes against humanity. Many of these so-called patriots were considered heroes when in fact it depended on whose side you are on. When you look at the Revolutionary War, you see the settlers overthrow the British and take full control of America. You hear the stories of Paul Revere and all of the other carefully scripted folklore and if you are White you should be ecstatic. But what if you are Black and the next step was slavery? What if you are a Native American and your history includes your people being slaughtered and your land taken away?

Then you are introduced to the Civil War and you hear conflicting stories of why the war was fought. Was it really about freedom of the slaves or was it an economic war (sounds familiar)? I have done research on Abraham Lincoln and believe he was a great leader. One of the best leadership books that I have ever read "Team of Rivals – The Political Genius of Abraham Lincoln" by Dolores Kearns gave me some great insight on working through difficult professional relationships to do what is best for everyone involved. In Lincoln, you see a man who is honest as possible and declares that if freeing the slaves is what is best for the Union, then that is what should be done, but if not then let them remain slaves. This was not something that I

99

learned in the classroom; this is something that I had to discover for myself. As a young student, you are carefully manipulated in the classroom. The curriculum is carefully crafted to keep the powers that be in charge and all others to continue to stay in their place.

Years later I would be introduced to the both Europe and the Soviet Union and their histories. I actually knew more about the Soviet Union than I did Black history until later in my high school years. I still remember Lenin, Stalin, Khrushev, and the some of the others. The funny part was that we would spend months on these foreign nations and then rush right through the contributions of Black America. Again, the subject we always spent the most time on was slavery. I have asked myself on numerous occasions why were our contributions so irrelevant to the educational system? Why did we need February the shortest month of the year for Black History Month instead of prioritizing the people who looked like us year-round?

The best history lesson that I ever received during my school years was Alex Haley's "Roots," and this was 1977, and I was a junior in high school. Alex Haley was a brilliant writer (later I would read the Autobiography of Malcolm X, easily the most important book of my life) and "Roots" finally gave us what we needed to see. Slavery without some mis-informed, prejudiced educator trying to make it seem as if it really didn't impact us for future generations. I can remember going back to school and many of the teachers really did not know what to do. Some of the brave ones talked about Roots and even assigned it, but the majority were lost and did not realize that this was a rare opportunity for them to really educate us about an important chapter of our history. Sometimes educators are locked into the curriculum and not able to really teach, others are locked into their mortgage and really don't' care, and then you have those that have a hatred for those who don't look like them.

Even today with the Internet and a surplus of information, you still see an absence of real teaching. I can't tell you how many students I encounter that can tell me what continent certain countries belong in. Many of us are still so misinformed about Africa and look at it with a sense of embarrassment. Africa is a great continent with a great history that needs to be discussed at length in the classroom.

Overall, we must begin to educate our children at home. We cannot rely on others to prioritize subjects that we know are important to their education. Learning about the accomplishments of people who look like you should be the cornerstone of any educational system. The definition of social studies is as follows; a course of study including geography, history, government, and sociology, taught in secondary and elementary schools. My question to the educational community of America is if this is the definition, then why many of you are failing in implementing the course of study. Why do we have children, particularly children of color, graduating high school, and they are deficient in geography, history (limited to learning about only certain cultures, particularly European dominated), government, sociology (what type of development of human society can take place without equality)? Again, what is the deal?

From day one I made sure my children were surrounded with books related to Black studies. They were required to read and issue their parents reports on the readings. There were hours of viewing documentaries like "Eyes on The Prize" and other Black studies. In the late '80s and '90s, I was the Chairman of the Youth Committee of the Rochdale Black Cultural Society (RBCS), an organization that offered programs for youth that taught them their history and brought in guest speakers. The RBCS has headed by Clara Hopkins a very committed and strong Black woman who I have a great amount of respect for. Other prestigious members included Richard Brown (RIP) and Betty Davis (RIP), both of whom were also very committed and knowledgeable. We brought in some highly respected Black historians, including Dr. Henry Clarke, Dr. Ivan Van Sertima, Dr. Frances Cress Welsing and some others. We also had programs for the youth, which included brining in speakers such as Sister

101

Souljah who left everyone speechless.

You cannot allow others to teach your children their history; that is a parent's job, and real parents do not allow others to do their jobs.

NCAA

"The National Collegiate Athletic Association (NCAA) is a voluntary organization through which the nation's colleges and universities govern their athletics programs. It is comprised of institutions, conferences, organizations and individuals committed to the best interests, education and athletics participation of student-athletes."   Does anyone really believe this bullshit? The NCAA is a corporation like Apple, American Express, and Microsoft that just happens to be in the business of governing amateur sports. My critique of the NCAA is not about some of the people who work for the organization because some people need jobs, and they have to do what they have to do. I am focusing on the mission of the organization itself. I have been working with college athletes my entire adult life, so I fully understand the organization in both theory and practice. Having observed them over the years, I strongly believe the organization is so out of touch with the world. Many of the rules and regulations are designed to make money for everyone, but the people who bring in the money. Listen to me very careful student athletes, parents, grandparents, aunts, uncles, cousins, sincere coaches, sincere advisors, sincere clergy, sincere educators, do not trust the NCAA. FUCK THE NCAA. Hear me again FUCK THE NCAA. They are profiting off of Black and Brown kids and have the unmitigated gall to make billions of dollars, and then suspend kids for taking coins. Any kid who is somewhat observant sees predominately White men living extremely well while they are eating in a cafeteria with no money in their pockets. Rules are explained to them that they are not to take anything from anyone or that is considered an infraction. If your uncle sends you a plane ticket to come home for the holidays, he has to let the school know because if it is not reported the student athlete is violating the rules. Really! What fucking business is it of the NCAA? The two sports that bring in the majority of the revenue for the NCAA and many of the universities are football and basketball. These two sports are dominated by Black athletes who at the end of the day are relegated to amateur status even though they bring in billions of dollars. Is there a contradiction somewhere or am I just crazy? Some of the coaches, athletic

103

directors, and school officials earn millions of dollars off of the backs of our children. Sound familiar? These student athletes are then asked to follow strict rules and guidelines and trust people who in many cases are only looking to make a profit at their expense. How many kids over the years have we seen that have been abandoned by colleges and universities because they have not met expectations? What happens to these kids? Some are lucky to transfer to another school while others have to return home with nothing to show for it. The NCAA, college universities, athletic directors, coaches, and others involved in college sports are PIMPS there is no other word for them. Let's take a closer look. PIMPS control where their workers live; they control what they eat; the workers are not allowed to talk or take anything from anybody without knowledge of the PIMP; the PIMPS control all of the money and only gives you what they want you to have; the PIMP controls the transportation; the PIMP punishes you if you do not follow the rules; when you no longer produce for the PIMP, they throw you into the street.

The NCAA/College System controls where the student athlete lives; they control what they eat; they are not allowed to talk to take anything without knowledge of the NCAA/College System; they control all of the money and only gives the student athlete what they want them to have; they control the transportation; the NCAA/College System punishes the student athlete if he/she does not follow the rules; when the student/athlete no longer produces for the NCAA/College System, they are thrown into the street.

There is a debate going on now during the COVID-19 pandemic about how students return to campuses or how do we conduct remote learning so that we do not miss a year. The NCAA, Conference Presidents, Athletic Directors, and others are meeting to discuss how do we get the college football and basketball seasons going so they don't miss out on the billons they take in each year. These sorry motherfuckers don't even have the decency to just cancel the season so that we can insure the health of everyone involved. They are plotting as always to take advantage of Black and Brown students to line their pockets. Listen people: FUCK THE NCAA! Do what is best for you. Use your common sense.

The bottom line is some of these university representatives are just as deadly as the neighborhood pusher. At the end of the day, it is all about money and not about the future of our children. I have witnessed some of the dumbest shit in my life that has been co-signed by the NCAA. I have seen children in need who are asked to go without because of stupid rules that make absolutely no sense. The irony of it all is that while some of these children suffer, coaches, athletic directors, boosters, and others have mastered the art of exploiting children and are making millions of dollars off of them.

Many of us are deceived when we see one of our kids making it big earning millions of dollars after signing a major professional contract. However, in the grand scheme of things, there is a very small percentage that actually makes it to the top. Many never graduate and leave the institution with nothing to show for it. In the end, if they have no value to the institution, they are abandoned, and most have no plan on what to do when this happens.

College sports regulated by the NCAA is big business for many in America. College football alone is an industry in Las Vegas where odds are laid, and bets are made similar to pro football. The only difference is the players in college football are not paid, but everyone else is paid well. College basketball is not far behind and again makes tremendous revenue for everyone involved.

While this is going on, the NCAA is busy looking for people who break the rules so they can levy punishment, including probation periods for schools and declaring student athletes ineligible. Their decisions are based on accumulating evidence, reviewing the evidence, and then making a decision. Like the real world, please understand in the end money talks and bullshit walks.

It starts with the AAU programs and the ranking of children athletes, which has become another issue in our communities. This is then is magnified by colleges and universities and the NCAA. In the end everyone is trying to make money off of our children's backs. They all misrepresent themselves and very few really have the genuine concern for our children.

In the end, we must do what is best for our children and that starts with being honest with them. When they are being recruited by colleges and universities and monitored by the NCAA, they are assets that will be used and abused. That is the reality of life. As one of my best friends BJ would say, "If you can't be used, then you are useless."

The NCAA and other institutions will always be lurking in the back looking to pounce on our children while others benefit from their talents. Student athletes be careful who you trust, and make good decisions about what you accept from adults. By no means should you ever go hungry, and if you really need assistance, try to find someone that is not affiliated with the educational institution or NCAA. In other words, call home. Yes, there are people in your community that will exploit you, but in most cases, they are not advertising themselves as a good will business.

The NCAA is a crooked organization looking to make money from suffering communities with the majority of its leadership being White males, sounds familiar. They take in a huge amount of money and have hoodwinked and exploited people of color for many years. We have to educate our youth to look at people for who they really are. The recruiters, coaches, athletic directors, and the NCAA all have the same thing in common and that is to use your talents to make money. You must educate yourself and become mature fast so you can use your talents to further your interests and better your family. Too many of our kids have been used, and its time we were paid for our talent. The time is now that college athletes were paid for their talent. No more freebies.

FUCK THE NCAA!

Corporate America (The Plantation)

When I think of corporate America, the first thing that comes to my mind is a plantation. I say this because like a plantation in order for the majority (just about everybody) of Black and Hispanic folks to advance (get ahead), you will have to suppress who you really are or to be honest to assimilate into the White culture. I am sure right now there are some of our folks who strongly believe they have advanced while staying true to themselves and in some rare cases this is true, but the majority have assimilated. I have seen this so many times in my life our people who forgot who they were when they got to the office. Some of them even changed their voices and chose not to speak with others of their race and culture. You all know who I am talking about. When you get to your office tomorrow after reading this, you will smile because they will appear right before you. These fools are trying so hard to prove that they are different so that they can be accepted into the master's house. In the end, they realize that they have hit a wall and that is as far as they are going.

Today there four CEO's among the largest 500 companies in the United States: Marvin Ellison of Lowe's, Kenneth Frazier of Merck, Roger Ferguson of TIAA, and Jade Zeitlin of Tapestry each has done an incredible job of climbing the corporate ladder. However, let's be clear, these men are exceptions to the rule. For most Blacks and Hispanics, they will be relegated to positions that are far from the top. They will see people of other races join the company at the same time but move up significantly faster than them. Some will become extremely frustrated and show their disapproval, which will prevent them from advancing. Others will assimilate with hopes of advancing and in some instances show some progress. Don't get me wrong; many of us have bills to pay and children to take care of, so we must do what is best for our families. However, we must find an acceptable medium of doing a quality job without giving up who we are.
I cannot tell you how many times I have had conversations with people who have revealed how frustrated they are in their positions and that race played a critical role in how they were

treated. How many times they felt disrespected and abused but tolerated it because of their mortgage and other bills that needed to be paid. Is it not healthy to work year after year under conditions you believe are unfair? What does this do your mind, your body, and your self esteem level? Do you really believe these corporate officers that are raking in millions of dollars care about the Black man in the mailroom?

From a commonsense perspective, I pose the question in what civilized culture would it be alright for hundreds of people to be fired while one or two people are issued bonuses of millions of dollars? How can anyone defend this action? This practice occurred during the global financial crisis (2007-2008). I was always taught that leaders lead by their actions. So again, I pose the question: what leader would terminate employees while accepting money that could be diverted to the employees and save jobs? My answer is a plantation owner. That is what many of the Corporate CEO's and their cronies are, plantation owners. Their goal is to have you work your butts off while they enjoy the fruits of your labor. They fully understand that you need your job, and they take full advantage of that. The sad part of this equation is that Blacks and Hispanics continue to stay on the bottom and not only have to deal with inferior wages, but also are treated as second-class employees. Many of us have to be very careful on how we wear our hair, the clothes we wear, and how we express ourselves. This is 2020, and we still cannot identify too closely with our heritage for fear of being ostracized. In most cases, they will not blatantly inform you, but they will get their message across.

In the late '90s and early 2000's, many companies-initiated diversity programs due to pressure from outside forces. In some cases, these programs brought more attention to the plight suffered by non-white employees, but for the most part they have not really changed the corporate dynamics, which still exists today. Many companies have become very sophisticated and know how to play the diversity game, while still maintaining their true identity. Again, today, particularly in these tough economic times, the emphasis is on maintaining employment for many, so it is easy for companies to maintain status quo. We may have missed our only chance to really push diversity where it could really mean seeing significant change in the hierarchy of corporate America. Think how different America would be if you were truly evaluated equally in the office, and race did not play a role? Non-whites would be in positions where they could make critical decisions and establish themselves as leaders. As leaders, they could change the overall corporate identity and ensure that all races have an equal opportunity to climb the corporate ladder.

We must invest in programs that steer our youth toward being successful entrepreneurs. These programs need to be taught by individuals that really understand all of the pitfalls that truly exist. When we look to open businesses in many cases, there will be additional obstacles that we must overcome that some other groups are not faced with. In many cases, some just don't want us to own a business or have the equal opportunity that they enjoy.

While racial segregation was a crime to humanity, it did teach Black America how to build for themselves. During the 1950s, 1960s and some of the 1970s, it was very common for us to see a high percentage of Black owned businesses. These businesses provided goods and services for our communities and a great deal of pride. In the 1980s, Black America started to push their way into Corporate America, and many thought they had arrived. The irony of the situation was there was a major trade off. While we had finally become a part of mainstream America, we lost so much of our identity and our culture. Many of us basically forgot where we came from in exchange for being accepted by White America.

Today we must start to rebuild on exactly what Black America should be. It should be self-sufficient, strong, able, confident, and BLACK. If one thing has been made clear to us in the last four years, it is that there is a large portion of America that still does not look at us as equals.

Our men and women need to form strong alliances and begin to rebuild our culture and our own economy where we can improve the living conditions of our people. I am not advocating separation, but it would be nice if we could finally be a force to reckon with. When you look at many of the items that you purchase and see "Made in China," I am sure the Chinese feel a sense of pride. They can identify with a country, a culture, and a people that continue to accomplish so much. Other cultures share this pride, but when you are Black no matter how much pride you take in working for one of these American corporations, while you may have played a role in their success, in the end you are the slave that just picked the cotton.

Malcolm and Martin (Leadership)

Martin Luther King, Jr. Quotes

"I knew that I could never again raise my voice against the violence of the oppressed in the ghettos without having first spoken clearly to the greatest purveyor of violence in the world today – my own government."
—*King, 1967*

"I am convinced that if we are to get on the right side of the world revolution, we as a nation must undergo a radical revolution of values."
—*King, 1967*

"There is a magnificent new militancy within the Negro community all across this nation. And I welcome this as a marvelous development. The Negro of America is saying he's determined to be free and he is militant enough to stand up."
—*King, 1963*

"Don't let anybody frighten you. We are not afraid of what we are doing... We, the disinherited of this land, we who have been oppressed so long, are tired of going through the long night of captivity."
—*King, 1955*

"Black men have slammed the door shut on a past of deadening passivity."
—*King, 1968*

Malcolm X quotes

"You can't separate peace from freedom because no one can be at peace unless he has his freedom."
—*Malcolm X, 1965*

"We can never get civil rights in America until our human rights are first restored. We will never be recognized as citizens until we are first recognized as humans."
—*Malcolm X, 1964*

"I believe in human beings, and that all human beings should be respected as such, regardless of their color."
—*Malcolm X, 1965*

"It is a disgrace for Negro leaders not to be able to submerge our "minor" differences in order to seek a common solution to a common problem posed by a common enemy."
—*Malcolm X, 1963*

"I have been convinced that some American whites do want to help cure the rampant racism which is on the path to destroying this country."
—*Malcolm X, 1964*

I think that few will argue that Martin Luther King Jr. and Malcolm X were the greatest Black leaders in American history. There has been so much research done on each independently, compared to each other, and as rivals. My thoughts and perspective will deal with them as a team. While they spent very little time together, the fact that they both were the leading figures of the Black Freedom Movement in the mid twentieth century, in my eyes, make them an elite team. The word team is defined as a group on the same side, and I think we will all agree that they were on the same side. While they had different strategies and had come from different backgrounds, they shared the goal of uplifting Black America.

The political consciousness of Black America influenced by both Martin and Malcolm has had its greatest growth since their deaths. Both men fully understood that the crisis of race relations has and always will dominate the arena of American life. Many historians over the years have tried to narrow them down to slogans, "I Have a Dream" for Martin, and "By Any Means

Necessary" for Malcolm. While both of these slogans were and are an essential part of their make-ups, they do not fully define who each was. Both men were very complex, yet both were very simple to understand. Their determination for Black America to gain freedom from oppression is the same as other oppressed peoples all over the world. They both organized movements that sought to end oppression with the understanding that there is no stopping point until you have fully secured full freedom.

During their lifetimes, both men received some of the best and worst press for men of their stature. It was very rare for those who did not know them to view them with objectivity, especially White America who saw them both as a threat to their existence. History has taught us that privileged groups rarely give up their privileges without resistance. During the mid twentieth century, America was at a crossroads and still not ready to accept Black Americans as equals. Unfortunately, not much has changed in 2020.

Both men need to be revisited in terms of the importance they have played in shaping the Black Freedom Movement and how it affects us today. Today, even though we have gained so much in technology, there is not a national movement in place fighting the inequality that still exists. Young men and women of African descent should be introduced to the teachings of both Malcolm X and Martin Luther King Jr. as a requirement. Malcolm's assertion of the cycle that "poor schools lead to poor jobs which leads to poor housing" and so on is as relevant today as it was during the 1960's. Martin's speech on the Vietnam War (1966) was probably one of the greatest speeches of all time, but never received the notoriety it deserved because he spoke out against America's involvement and the loss of innocent lives. When you look at the quotes I have listed above, you see them as relevant today as they were fifty years ago. Both men had visions of a great Black America, which we still have not achieved in 2020.

While Malcolm and Martin came from two very different backgrounds, they managed to form many of the same ideologies before their assassinations. Before their deaths, they had gained the insight of Black America's struggle in America and how it related to Africa, Asia, and other parts of the world. Both men were successful at elevating the role of Black America from a civil rights battle to a human rights struggle. By internationalizing the problem, both men elevated their status and became world leaders that America could no longer control. While their strategies were different, their goals were the same, to bring the plight of Black America to the world stage. Many would say that this is what ultimately led to their deaths.

Both men were in transition and had displayed a huge amount of maturity, wisdom, and intelligence when their lives were taken from them at the young age of thirty-nine. Both men were master orators with the ability to deliver their messages that could easily be understood on all educational levels. Both lived under the microscope of America that created a climate that ultimately led to their assassinations and took the wind out of the Black Freedom Movement.

Effective leadership is one of the most important ingredients for a successful society. The fact that Malcolm and Martin both were products of racist America in the mid-twentieth century allowed America to pick their poison, and they were delighted in some cases to choose Martin, because to them he represented the best case for them to continue to stay in control. Both were misunderstood and always will be for various reasons; however, they will always be the greatest leaders of our lifetime.

The untimely deaths of both Malcolm and Martin were tragic, and Black America has never recovered from their losses. Let me emphasize I mean no disrespect to anyone, but one major question I pose is where would Black America be if they had lived longer lives and had the opportunity to work as a team?

Che Guevara, Black Panther Party, and George Jackson

Great leadership influenced a lot of my life. I have spent a great deal of my adult life introducing young people to strong independent leaders who have given their lives for people of color.

No one embodies this more than Che Guevara. Che was arguably the greatest revolutionary of the twenty first century. All who truly envision a world of equality should study his dedication and commitment to people of color worldwide. Many college and universities now offer courses on Che, but like Malcolm and Martin, Che has been reduced to a popular tee shirt and other memorabilia. To truly understand the importance of Che Guevara is to look at how much time he spent devoted to uplifting people of color. He led by example, including his honesty, which at times struck fear in his detractors. Che was both the soldier and the general, and unlike many so-called leaders today, practiced what he preached.

Like Martin and Malcolm, Che was assassinated at the age of thirty-nine. Che was well on his way to creating change worldwide, and it would have benefitted humanity if he had the opportunity to complete his mission.

The Black Panther Party led by Huey P. Newton and Bobby Seales was a breath of fresh air for many in the Black community in the '60s. The Black Panther Party demonstrated that Blacks could stand against the establishment on its own terms, albeit at the risk of death, and that demonstration marked a new stage of evolution in the Black Liberation movement. Many Blacks had not witnessed their own standing up against the establishment the way these young brothers and sisters did. Knowing what we know today, the facts state that the Party was unfairly manipulated, infiltrated, and many lives were lost due to an establishment who we all know never plays fair. The party stood for justice for its people and many paid the ultimate price.

Today there is an absence of a movement like the Black Panther

Party. Many young people are misguided and have been led astray by poor leadership and sell-outs whose only interest is their personal gain. Young people are calling out for strong leadership, but the question is will we answer the call? I love the Black Lives Matter Movement and believe they have done a great job of organizing and implementing a strong agenda. We must establish our own strong Black corporate America where we can begin to control our own destiny and not always wait for others to decide to include us. I am not insinuating that others cannot be a part of this process, but merely stating that we are the minority in corporate America today, and there has to become a time when we are the majority for some firms that we control. Yes, we have to continue our grassroots movements and other organizational programs, but we have to operate and patronage our own businesses if we are going to control our destiny.

George Jackson was one of the great writers and visionaries of his time. His two most famous works include "Soledad Brother" and "Blood in my Eye." George was a legendary figure in the prison system in the early '70s whose writings are as relevant today as they were then. George was well on his way to establishing himself as one of the great revolutionaries of our time. Prison guards killed George in 1971, in what many consider an execution of a man who had gained enormous popularity for his views.

I share many things in common with George, including the same birthday (September 23rd), green eyes, and many of the same views on humanity. George is a lot like one of my closest friends (brother) currently serving an unjust sentence because of his ability to organize and refusal to be broken. We all are freedom fighters with a mission to uplift our people. George is important to me because like many of my contemporaries, we have family, colleagues, and friends in the prison system. We must begin to create a stronger bridge from prison back to society, and George Jackson is the perfect example of someone, like Malcolm, who expanded his mind and vision behind bars.

Lastly, I wear several tattoos, including Che Guevara, George Jackson, and of course El Hajji Malik Shabazz (Malcolm X), sorry no mermaids for me. They'll never count me among the broken men!

Intellectual Elitism vs. Common Sense

I have encountered many people over the years with various degrees from some of the most prestigious institutions in the world. I have also spent a great deal of time with some people with a high degree of common sense who have never grazed a college campus. If you were to ask me which group that I had a higher degree of respect, for it would be the latter. While I would be the first to admit that having a degree from one of these institutions will open up a lot of doors for you, in many ways some of these people developed a sense of superiority in their academic travels. I also have witnessed many academics who could not think for themselves and were really only brilliant in their fields. On the other hand, I have spent time with some people who were less educated but who could actually think and problem solve.

Some of the best advice that I ever received usually came from those who were not doing well at the time or had survived one or more tough situations. Coming from a tough neighborhood, many people are down on their luck and their only means of survival is using their mind and being creative. They have to create ways to earn money and keep a roof over their heads. "Necessity is the Mother of Invention" is a saying that I heard so much growing up, and to be honest I never thought much of it until I was in a tight spot as a teen. Being a good friend, I had loaned my partner some money. Now, for those of you that may not understand, the word loan is misused in the hood everyday. So in other words there is a strong possibility that I am not going to get this money back or I am not going get all of it, or I am not going to get it back when you said I would. So, knowing this I knew I had to find another way after I made the gift, I meant loan. So, my next move was to take what I had and do what needed to do and that is what I did, plain and simple. I had to think on my feet; there was no book for me to read to solve this dilemma. It worked out for me only because I used common sense and made a well thought out timely decision. One more day and I would not have made it.

Analyzing the situation, the so-called intellectual would think

119

that my partner would have all the money on time, because that is what we agreed to. Common sense says that if this motherfucker is getting money from me, he probably is in a bind and one of the first laws of the streets is that if you give a <u>partner</u> money, regardless of what is agreed to, be prepared to take it as a loss and move on, no hard feelings. I have been on both sides of the fence, and I am all right with it, even though I have lost far more than I have gained. As Chris Brown would say, "Chalk it up to Deuces." Most of the time people that are the closet to you will let you down. In my life there are very few people I have disappointed, but there are a few, and it really bothers me. I like to be thought of as dependable, and not a day goes that it doesn't cross my mind that I have not met expectations. I apologize to those few and haven't given up on fulfilling my shortcomings.

Intellectual Elitism is a prejudice that divides people. It destroys humanity and makes most of those who have encountered it feel inferior. People who make others believe they are superior because they have amassed a certain level of education usually are deficient in some other area trust me. You so-called intellectuals need to understand while you may be brilliant in your field, there are so many other parts of life. There are millions of people in this world who have made some of the greatest contributions to society without having spent a day in a college classroom. I salute those of you who have completed this mission but keep it in perspective. It does not make you a better person or raise your level on the human totem pole. If this is you, and you practice elitism of any kind, you are as guilty as the biggest racist in the world.

My Uncle Cooper is one of the least educated people that I have ever met, but the skill level he posses to fix things is amazing. I have watched him time and time again fix things without a manual and it totally amazes me. He also has said something's that have made a whole lot of sense. He is in his 90's and still fixing things.

If there were a war between Intellectual Elitism and Common

Sense, Intellectual Elitism would devise a plan to eliminate Common Sense because of selfishness and the feeling of superiority. Common Sense Team would devise a plan to make peace with Intellectual Elitism because Common Sense would realize that both working together would benefit all involved.

Next time use common sense!

Politicians

Over the years, I have had to deal with politicians on several different levels. Sometimes to try and secure funding for different programs, sometimes when an emergency situation has happened, and there are always the times when they are trying to secure support. Let me be clear never in my life have I personally had any political ambitions. I have always been clear about that and always will be. My first lesson in dealing with politicians taught me well, and after that I always knew that they had to lie in order to make everyone content. You notice that I used the word content and not happy. Politicians have to lie because they cannot make everyone happy. Are there some exceptions to the rule, probably yes, but I doubt it? I know that is a contradiction, but when you start talking politics this is what happens.

I have witnessed politicians and their staffs blatantly lie again and again. The sad part of it all is that some of these staff members know part of their jobs is to lie. When they take these positions part of their job descriptions is to do whatever is necessary to keep their representative in power. How many times have we seen a politician in trouble over the years? Many take on this responsibility knowing full well that they cannot meet the high standard of representing the people. I will admit being a politician is a tall order because in some cases you are being asked to be as close to perfect as possible.

Another issue that affects politicians is that for all of the power that you supposedly have, in most cases, there is not a high salary that goes with it. To put it in perspective, even being the President of the United States is not a high paying job considering how much you have to deal with. So, when people take on these positions and start to feel powerful, it is only a matter of time before they crave the money that they believe should go with it. The next thing that happens is that deals start to take place and money starts to appear from constituents who need favors. Don't get me wrong; there are some people who go into politics with good intentions, but very few, if any, leave that way. There are just too many things going on for these so-called public figures to stay 100% honest. Temptation is a bitch and sometimes, as we all know, it is not even money, there are other things that pull you across that line.

Part of the issue here in America is that in the Black community we have been brainwashed into being loyal to the Democratic Party. While in most cases the Democratic Party is the lesser of two evils, the fact remains that they take the Black vote for granted. Over the years, the Black community has been very loyal to the Democratic Party, but we have seen little improvement in our communities. We are still not equal in America, and right now things are worse than ever. There is a huge amount of unemployed Black and Hispanic Americans that see no sign of hope. We have limited resources and our schools are in poor condition. Violence in our communities is at an all time high, and good people are losing their homes. Our political representation has not done a great job of creating positive change. Are they totally to blame? Absolutely not, but they are significant part of the problem.

Today, I like the young politicians like Alexandria Ocasio-Cortez, Ilhan Omar, Ayanna Pressley, Rhashida Talib, and some others. I think it is time for a woman President. I like the work of the Black Lives Matter Movement and other organizations and the energy of the young people in streets and on social media. The COVID-19 pandemic has forced people to take their lives more seriously. I like that all races have attended the recent protests after the George Floyd murder. It gives us some hope, not trust but hope.

There are a few politicians that I really have a problem with and on top of that list is Tim Scott and Ben Carson. Let me be clear I have no loyalty to any political party and there have been times I did not vote at all. I usually side with the Democratic Party but have voted for an independent on several occasions. In my opinion, these two have really embarrassed themselves to a point they can never hold their heads high again. Tim Scott let a group of White senators march him out to speak on a watered-down police reform bill that was a complete joke. You would have thought that he never heard the name George Floyd. In my mind, I can see Tim and Ben holding Harriet Tubman down waiting for the slave master to get there.

In Malcolm X's famous speech delivered in 1963, "The Ballard or the Bullet," Malcolm makes the following statements that are as relevant today as it was in 1963. I have deleted a few lines from the speech below because it was not relevant. With an election around the corner, it would be wise for us to revisit Brother Malcolm X (see below):

The Ballard or the Bullet

"I say again, I'm not anti-Democrat, I'm not anti-Republican, I'm not anti-anything. I'm just questioning their sincerity, and some of the strategy that they've been using on our people by promising them promises that they don't intend to keep. When you keep the Democrats in power, you're keeping the Dixiecrats in power. A vote for a Democrat is a vote for a Dixiecrat. That's why, in 1964, it's time now for you and me to become more politically mature and realize what the ballot is for; what we're supposed to get when we cast a ballot; and that if we don't cast a ballot, it's going to end up in a situation where we're going to have to cast a bullet. It's either a ballot or a bullet."

"The political philosophy of black nationalism means that the black man should control the politics and the politicians in his own community; no more. The black man in the black community has to be re-educated into the science of politics so he will know what politics is supposed to bring him in return. Don't be throwing out any ballots. A ballot is like a bullet. You don't throw your ballots until you see a target, and if that target is not within your reach, keep your ballot in your pocket."

As I read and listen to Malcolm, I see how often we have let our political representatives off lightly. I say this with little hesitation; we must hold them accountable for their actions. If you do not have the best intentions for our people, then do not run for office. Our communities are a mess; we need the best leadership possible in order to turn it around. That means we need committed people who fully understand that this job does not a pay well and requires a lot of overtime.

The criteria have been set, only those qualified need to apply!

Presidents in My Lifetime

My life started out with **John F. Kennedy,** the thirty-fifth
president. JFK as he is commonly known was a special man in
many ways. Kennedy is the only Catholic, and the first Irish
American, president. Major events during his presidency
included the Bay of Pigs Invasion and the Cuban Missile Crisis.
JFK is also known for leading the Space Race and contributing to
Civil Rights Movement. JFK also was heavily involved in the
early stages of the Vietnam War. He still is the only president to
have won a Pulitzer Prize, so his talents were many. Even though
I was only three when he died, I constantly saw his picture in the
many homes that I ventured into in my life. It was very common
to see JFK hanging next to Martin Luther King Jr. on the walls of
Black families in the hood. JFK has more appeal then all of the
other White Presidents of my lifetime. Later after completing
additional research, he may have gotten more credit than he
deserved for the Civil Rights Movement but still kept his respect.
My admiration of JFK was based more on how he carried
himself. He was very stylish and a great speaker, so he was
capable of attracting support from both men and women and
people from all races. Don't get me wrong, he had his enemies as
well as evidenced by his assassination, but overall remains one of
America's most popular presidents. JFK also had more of a
movie star appeal, which attracted a fan base no other president
before him had enjoyed. Part of JFK's popularity can also be
contributed to his wife Jackie, who changed the role of the First
Lady and become an icon herself. Growing up Black in America
you still have a great deal of respect for the presidency, and JFK
made it a lot easier because at least on the surface he appeared to
be on our side. Some will argue the point and say like Lincoln he
did what was best for the United States and if that meant
supporting the Civil Rights Movement then that is what he did. If
it meant not, then that is the road he would have taken. Maybe
because we just like him, we will give him a pass and that is all
right with me.

Lyndon Baines Johnson or LBJ was the exact opposite of Kennedy. LBJ was not a style icon and did not have the massive appeal of JFK, including his popularity with women. Johnson a die-hard Texas Democrat served six years as president, including being elected in 1964. After taking over for Kennedy after his assassination, Johnson also played a role in the Civil Right Movement and is credited with passing the Civil Rights Act of 1964. While these important legislations played some role in advancing the rights of Blacks, in many ways most still endured tough times during this period. In addition to his domestic policies, LBJ's major obstacle would come from the Vietnam War and the leadership role he played, including increasing the number of troops. As the United States involvement increased in the war, LBJ's popularity plummeted. Many have mixed views on the LBJ presidency, and like JFK he may have received credit that he did not deserve regarding the Civil Rights Movement, but the Vietnam War will always be his albatross.

Richard Millhouse Nixon was the thirty-seventh president of the United States and contrary to what most would think one of my favorites. I spent a great deal of time researching Nixon when I was in school to do several reports in the early '70s. This research taught me a great deal about government including the House, Senate, Judicial, and the Executive Branches. I also was introduced to the voting process and sadly the impeachment process as well. Nixon was a Quaker that came from a very poor childhood, but somehow became president. Nixon or Tricky Dick as he is commonly referred to was different than many of the White men that I encountered growing up. He just seemed to be more straight forward and you kind of knew where you stood. In the Black community you were taught that Nixon was a Republican and that you were a Democrat and that made him the enemy. The reality was that there was not much difference in how both major political parties would treat the Black Community. We were a voting block that both parties needed to win, so like anything else promises would be made and very few kept. After the election, we would still not be equal with the rest of America. With Nixon, we had a better understanding of where

127

the Black Community stood. It was not in front of the line, but we had a spot. It was up to us how we moved along; just keep your ducks in a row.

When Watergate broke, we were not as affected as White America. The term *Watergate* has come to encompass an array of illegal and secret activities undertaken by members of the Nixon administration that ultimately led to his impeachment (resignation). I can remember listening to adults discussing Watergate in the hood and how many understood that it was politics and power and how people would do whatever they needed to do to win. The reaction at school with many of the teachers who were White was like he personally committed a sin. I can say it was another part of history that divided race and because we both saw it so differently.

Overall, Nixon's presidency will be remembered for Watergate, but his work in foreign policy including visiting China, Treaty Negotiations with the Soviet Union, and ending the Vietnam War were parts of my education that I somehow still remember. I would have to admit that Nixon or in my case Tricky Dick had an affect on me. He was the main topic of conversation for a long time and may have introduced a lot of people to the inside world of politics. Black America was still on the outside looking in, but Nixon pulled up the shade.

Gerald Ford followed Nixon after his resignation. I don't have much to say about Ford. I remember that he is the only president who was not elected, taking over for Nixon after Watergate. Ford also pardoned Richard Nixon. In his defense, I probably would have done the same thing.

Jimmy Carter was the thirty-ninth president and like some of my family was born and raised in Georgia. When I think of Jimmy Carter, I have thoughts of a very good man. I really believe that he wanted to do some great things, but his misfortune was Iranian Hostage Crisis where American lives were lost. Still to this day Jimmy Carter has been a major advocate for Human Rights. Together with his wife Rosalyn, they continue to support many charities and non-profit organizations supporting Human Rights.

I remember **Ronald Reagan** as an actor in some of the old films my brother would make me watch growing up. In Regan, I saw what White America thought the epitome of their race was. He was loyal to his base, which included all classes of White America that took much pride in his presidency. Reagan's policies, including "Reaganomics," changed how America would move forward including re-establishing itself as the premier world power. Reagan was known as the "Gipper," and his role in the "Cold War" established him as a different kind of leader.

Like Nixon, we knew where we stood with Reagan. We understood he would protect his base and do everything in his power to get them what they needed. We knew the Black community would be treated like second class citizens but probably treated better than the Communists nations he despised. Reagan was an American, and he truly believed in America. Reagan was totally against affirmative action and some other programs designed to support people of color.

Whether you call him the Gipper, the Great Communicator, or the Teflon President, Ronald Reagan is widely understood in American history as one of the most popular presidents. In the hood most of us were happy when the Reagan era ended. No disrespect to his legacy; he followed the plan perfectly; the plan just did not include us.

George H.W. Bush is another president with less fanfare. His presidency was quiet and without any major event to define it. In America's eyes, he was following Ronald Reagan, not an easy task by any means. Bush did exactly enough and that is about all you can say. Everyone was just waiting to see who would be next.

Bill Clinton was a breath of fresh air to America and especially for people of color. Let me be clear, I believe that Bill Clinton is a very good man who may have made a couple of bad decisions. No matter who you are you will do something one day that you wish you didn't do. Auntie always told me that the key to all is that the good you do must outweigh the bad you do and the more it does the better chance you have. I still believe that, and it works for me. I believe the good Bill Clinton has done far outweighs the bad.

During the Clinton era, my youth organization had the resources to really provide programs. These were the years we had trips, equipment, supplies, clothing, and food. You want to change America come up with the money to clothe and feed it. In the Clinton era, our kids ate. That is a good way to measure the success of a President to me. If the elderly and youth are eating, a country is being run well.

On paper, they will say Clinton left office with the highest end-of-office approval rating of any U.S. president since World War II Since then, he has been involved in public speaking and humanitarian work. Clinton created the William J. Clinton Foundation to promote and address international causes such as treatment and prevention of HIV/AIDS and global warming.

In the hood, they will say Bill Clinton gave us the best shot we had up until then to really get somewhere. Bill was well received in the Black community and in some ways he really understood. Even Hilary I believe understands; I think sometimes the job pulls you another way. However, before you get pulled too far, you have to straighten yourself out. The Clinton's are good people, but they are also politicians and that makes things hard sometimes. I believe they do the right thing seven out of ten times, but there are the few times when, I will leave it there.

George W. Bush will probably be defined most by September 11th Terrorist Attacks (911). It is the event that will always be linked to his presidency. While flooded with domestic issues

130

including healthcare, immigration, Social Security, and the economy, Bush waged wars with both Iraq and Afghanistan after the attacks. The cost of the wars and the toll on human lives being lost had a significant affect on the Bush presidency.

In the Black community, we again knew that we did not have a firm supporter in the White House. George Bush like those before him had his constituency, and he would do everything in his power to protect it.

Hurricane Katrina was a horrible event in the history of America, as we know it. We can only imagine what some of those people went through. I do not think that Bush had anything to do with the disaster and believe that he sincerely wished that no one came to any harm. His error probably came from somebody else who didn't do their job and ultimately, he has to take the blame. However, Bush's major error was how he treated the Black community from the start. Most of us felt unwanted and unprotected in our own country. Resources were not made available to us and many of us saw a decline in overall services. Hurricane Katrina was just more ammunition to prove the double standard.

Bush was not many of things that people made him out to be and he definitely was not stupid. He was tough and defiant at times and I guess he had to be. I just would have preferred if he was fairer when it came to human rights.

Barack Hussein Obama is a very special person. In my personal opinion, he was too good of a person to be president. Let me be clear; he was more than qualified, in fact brilliant, and was very smooth. My opinion is based on the fact that he really cares about people in general, and when you are president in most cases, there are groups or a group that you specifically give preferential treatment to. Obama is a sincere man who truly tried to represent all of the people. If I were president, I would have given preferential treatment to the Black and Hispanic communities. I truly believe we deserved it; after all of the bullshit we have been

131

through in building America, I would have abused the power.

Obama's presidency was a huge success, and what he did for Black America could never be measured, but it was amazing. What he means to Black America, poor people, and the world overall is still felt and respected. Obama has given so many people hope in a time when it is so easy to give up. Obama has given so many men, particularly Black men, with no male role model a firsthand look of how a father, husband, businesses person, and man conducts himself.

Michelle, our amazing First Lady has also done an outstanding job of revolutionizing the role. While Jackie Kennedy broke the standard, Michelle has taken it to a whole new level. The beauty, confidence, intelligence, and grace she displays on a regular basis are the lessons for women of all races to embrace.

The Obama's family is complete with two excellent parents and two beautiful daughters that have put their personal lives on display for the world to view. We will watch them grow as individuals and as a family, and they all will make us proud because they are special people. Barack Hussein Obama was the forty-fourth president of the United States of America, a Black man. He has made us all proud!

In the end, I still believe that there is no difference in politics and crime. Most of us have been brainwashed into accepting politics into our lives because we have been sold on America as a democracy. I challenge you to do your research where you will find a very different story. I have always been fascinated by the U.S. Presidency. I chose to write about it because living in America you are brainwashed on the red, white, and blue and its leaders. America is like any other organized crime family; its goal is to remain in power.

Donald Trump is our forty-fifth president and so far in my lifetime all of the people who have held the office have been White men with the exception of Obama, so it is the norm. I don't have much to say about him nor do I have a problem with him. However, I will make one critical point. DT represents his base and is very honest about it. If you know that and you are not part of his base, then you know where you stand.

Favors

A favor is defined as; *A gracious, friendly, or obliging act that is freely granted.*

In "Carlito's Way," a very popular urban movie of the '90s, Al Pacino (one of my favorite actors) plays a major drug dealer released from prison and trying to get his life together. Although this role is fictional, it is a reality in many urban communities in America. Contrary to popular belief, when most return from prison they want to end all drama and move on with their lives. The problems occur when they cannot step back into society and attempt to be a functional part of it. They will never be given a fair shot at redemption, which ultimately will lead them back into a life of crime or poor decisions. This is not an excuse; it is a reality, and one I have witnessed my entire life.

In the film Carlito (Pacino) says to one of his associates, *"A favor will kill you faster than a bullet."* As I analyze this line, it speaks volumes to the dilemma that faces many in the hood. While many of us are facing an uphill battle, we have to establish in our minds that we have to find a way to make things better for ourselves. We cannot rely on others, particularly our family and friends to bail us out every time we face adversity. Many times, when others loan us money or do some other task, it puts them in a bad position. They may tell you it is cool, and may even have the resources, but in the long run it affects them and ultimately the relationship that you share. I know there are times when you need help, but you have to make those times scarce. Many of us will have to find a way out of whatever mess we created for ourselves.

Black men and other men of color you already know that the deck is stacked against you, so it is crucial that you make good decisions. If you decide to pursue a life of crime and fail, you cannot expect others to bend over backwards when you return from prison. If you decide to have unprotected sex, then you must assume the role of a father, including the financial responsibility. If you continue to live in the home with your parents (in most cases the mother), then you have to find employment and contribute to the household expenses. This includes many of you fake professional athletes that are wasting time going back and forth overseas when you know you are not making any real money. If you move in with your girlfriend and children (especially those under Section Eight), you should find employment and contribute to the household and provide emotional support so that you both can move forward and be able to run a home without assistance. On a lesser note, many of you need to get your own car or take the bus; you never wash it or put the gas back anyway.

Many of the young people I encounter are reluctant to take jobs at McDonalds, Burger King, and some of the other fast food establishments. We have created this false identity that has been exasperated by peer pressure. Many of our people really believe that they are too good to take a job because of what others will think. This is a lot of bullshit that needs to be put to rest immediately. Sometimes you have to do what you have to do. It does not mean you will be there forever, but in order to live in an America, you must have money. If I had to, I would shovel shit in a white suit if that would pay the bills! That is what a man does for his family and loved ones. Many of you have never been taught nor had a role model, but you have to get pass that and grow into being a man.

We can no longer expect favors; everyone must pull their weight. Besides, most of the people who ask for favors are never in position to grant one. Next time just say no. I know it may be difficult, but by saying no you may be doing the person a favor!

25 Questions

This chapter is dedicated to asking some questions that one day should be answered.

1. Why did Denzel Washington and Halle Berry both win Academy Awards for negative Black characters in "Training Day" and "Monster's Ball" when they both deserved the awards for other performances, including "Malcolm X" and "Hurricane" for Denzel and "Losing Isaiah" for Halle?

2. What is the significance or coincidence to Martin Luther King Jr., Malcolm X, and Che Guevara all being assassinated at age thirty-nine (39)?

3. Organized dogfighting has been going on since the beginning of time, why did Michael Vick need to be the poster boy for this atrocity?

4. Why does the United States continue to use the Electoral College voting system for President, when most citizens would prefer a direct election (popular vote)?

5. With the advancement in technology (DNA) involving criminal investigations, why hasn't someone been arrested in both the assassinations of both Tupac and Biggie?

6. When history is taught in schools, why does the curriculum address the key leaders as the" Founding Fathers" when they were slave owners for Blacks? Does this mean they were both our fathers and our masters?

7. Why does America promote rehabilitation, when we fully understand that one mistake will prevent you from ever being given a second chance in most cases?

8. Why is there so much corruption in government, but yet they are still allowed to judge private citizens and charge taxes?

9. How can anyone ever really expect Black America to forget or forgive the era of "Slavery"? Should we?

10. When doesn't race play a role?

11. Have you ever seen White America be more disrespectful

136

to a President than they were to President Obama?

12. In my lifetime, Veterans, particularly from Vietnam and some of the smaller wars are not the same when they return. Is the price of war worth it?

13. Does the American government continue to punish Cuba because they would like to control it?

14. How could any jury in the Rodney King trial come back with any verdict but guilty?

15. Why are the Native Americans being forced to live on reservations to retain land?

16. Why are our schools filled with teachers who should have been removed already?

17. Why did America allow New Orleans to be flooded?

18. What happened to television? And what is realistic about reality television?

19. Why aren't more Black and Hispanic men allowed to teach kindergarten, first, and second grades?

20. Why are so many of our young people saddled with loans for education when education is free in other countries?

21. Why does an organization like Sallie Mae even exist? They clearly are a loan shark for the government who clearly exploit the college experience.

22. How much money does America owe us (Black America) for our labor?

23. Where are all of the singing groups? In the '60s, '70s, and '80s, we were flooded with singing groups where are they now, and why have we turned to individual artists as our preferred entertainment?

24. Does an honest politician exist?

25. Why is there so much money spent on elections?

Fifty Things I have Learned

1. Good people do bad things.
2. That church is not for everybody, and no one should attempt to push it on others.
3. Mothers are the most important people on earth, but if you have a father too, you usually are better prepared for life.
4. That everyone has a price, maybe your price is zero, but you have a price.
5. You should live together before you get married.
6. Men that chose to leave a woman, particularly when children are involved, should only take their personal possessions. Everything else stays.
7. In life you give someone three strikes and then you move on. If you stay longer, you get what you deserve. In fact, tread lightly after they get two.
8. Politicians are not paid well, so they have to find a way to make money.
9. Clergy are human just like you and are no closer to Heaven than anybody else.
10. Many teachers do not like the students they are teaching.
11. People (men and women) who don't want to get pregnant wear condoms. No excuses.
12. College is overrated for some, but when applied properly, makes a big difference.
13. White people have and always will set up organizations that so call help people of color, but in the end, it was and always will be about money.
14. Most police are scared of the people they are policing.
15. Litter is the first sign that a community is changing for the worst.
16. Black Slavery in America was the biggest crime the world has ever witnessed, nothing else comes close.
17. People who are always late, you fill in the blanks.
18. Common sense is the difference-maker for reasonable people.
19. History, including the Bible, is full of lies point blank but has been extremely effective in molding the minds of all

people.

20. Some junkies and alcoholics are more honorable than some people with no addictions.
21. Drugs will be here forever, along with alcohol, prostitution, and gambling, and most people are happy about that.
22. Women are better people than men, but the worst woman is _not_ better than the worst man.
23. Sunday has always been the best day of the week for me. It is the day that reminds me of my Aunt.
24. Some people should marry for money, not most but some.
25. Rape is the worst crime you can commit.
26. Usually, the worst things happen after 12:00am for both men and women, but for women, it can be worst.
27. Judge people by their intentions, not the results, you cannot control everything that will happen, but be clear of what they intended.
28. Middle School is the beginning of who you really are, other things will alter your identity, but this is where it starts.
29. Money changes people, but love changes them more.
30. I do not have any White friends, but I do have friends that are White, there is a difference.
31. When things really get bad, you are all by yourself. People will tell you some encouraging things, but they have their own problems.
32. Two things happen in a relationship, the more you see, the more you like, or the opposite, the more you see, the less you like. Time is honest.
33. The capitalist system is designed to use you up in the prime years of your life while you make somebody else rich. Some may live pretty well compared to the average person, but in the end, you still have been used.
34. I grew up in NYC, and our family never had a car, so my brother and I learned early how to travel without one on buses and trains throughout the city. It makes a big difference in your life; we saw so much more.
35. You never ever put that money back when you use it. It is

just the way life pans out.

36. When one of my friends drowned after we snuck into the local pool in my early teens, it made me follow rules more closely. Since that day I never play in water.

37. Women have never been treated as equals by White men, but you can never compare it to being Black or Hispanic.

38. Many people have become their business cards. That is not who you are. It is what you do to earn a living.

39. Some adults really can't read. It is sad but true.

40. Skin color will always matter; nobody can deny that. It matters, even more when money is involved.

41. If you ass bet (have no money), you deserve what you get.

42. Some of those guns are not loaded. Some of you are playing a dangerous game.

43. Self-discipline is the most important trait you can own. It is even more effective if you will punish yourself.

44. Adults should never get high with children. Drugs and alcohol make everyone equal.

45. Weddings are more important to women. Most men could do without it.

46. Opposites attract, is a foolish statement. People like people who are like them. My wife and I are very similar in more ways than we are different. It would not work any other way.

47. Once you make it home stay in. If you come back out, you get what you deserve. It can wait until tomorrow.

48. Men can cry in public depending on the situation but never accept a tissue. In fact, wipe your tears with your hand.

49. Be open to change; today we have to be more receptive to the LBGTQ community; they are people like everyone else. They are also extremely talented.

50. Never tell someone you have a headache. That is your problem, and it is up to you how you deal with it.

Part Four – Real Nigga

Street Talk (The Word Nigger/Nigga)

Not a day goes by that I do not hear the word nigger or nigga. In fact, I use the word on a regular basis. The word has caused a major controversy for many different reasons.
According to Arthur K. Spears. (Diverse Issues in Higher Education, 2006)

In many African American neighborhoods, nigga is simply the most common term used to refer to any male, of any race or ethnicity. Increasingly, the term has been applied to any person, male or female. "Where y'all niggas goin?" is said with no self-consciousness or animosity to a group of women, for the routine purpose of obtaining information. The point: Nigga is evaluatively neutral in terms of its inherent meaning; it may express positive, neutral or negative attitudes.

While Kevin Cato observes:

For instance, a show on Black Entertainment Television, a cable network aimed at a Black audience, described the word nigger as a "term of endearment."

In the African American community, the word nigga (not nigger) brings out feelings of pride" (Davis 1). Here the word evokes a sense of community and oneness among Black people. Many teens I interviewed felt that the word had no power when used amongst friends, but when used among white people the word took on a completely different meaning. In fact, comedian Alex Thomas on BET stated, "I still better not hear no white boy say that to me. I hear a white boy say that to me, it means 'White boy, you gonna get your ass beat.'

I have chosen to offer a brief history of the word nigger/nigga because so many people have different opinions concerning its usage. As we move forward, I will use the word nigga instead of

141

nigger because I feel great pride and admiration for my sisters and brothers and strongly believe that the word is part of our culture.

While I fully understand that there are some people that will strongly disagree, I respect their opinions and hope they can do the same for me. I am a Black man of a certain age who has lived a full life and have spent almost my entire life working in Black communities assisting children and families. I have formed my opinion based on my life experiences and through discussions with people I thoroughly respect. While I fully understand that this will be ammunition for some people to attack me and my work, I stand one hundred percent by what I have written.

I have used the word in both formal and informal conversations to express my thoughts. I have used it amongst the educated, uneducated, adults and children. There are times when I greet young people by saying "what's up my nigga," and when I say it, I feel a sense of pride and belonging.

While I know that other races use the word, I strongly believe they shouldn't. It is our word to use and no one else's. In my lifelong studies, I believe the Hispanic community who I consider our direct brothers and sisters are the only group who I am not offended when they use the word. The Black and Hispanic communities are all one and if you do enough research and you should, you will understand we are all of the same Diaspora. I am fully aware of the negative connotations that come with the word, but like the slavery period, we should hold on to it forever. I understand that other groups as well as the Black community will use it in a negative manner, but we can't police the use of the word. If we ask our young people not to us the word, we are not being realistic and creating more confusion. The word nigga is not going away, and it shouldn't. In fact, it bothers me that when I type it comes up as spelled incorrectly. Just like us the word is strong and has multiple meanings and both strengths and weaknesses. The word is a survivor and has been through so much but has managed to stay relevant. Sounds familiar to a group of people in history.

I can remember several years ago when Jay-Z appeared on Oprah and they had the discussion on the use of the word "nigga" and agreed to disagree. I thought this was great for the Black community that two highly respected individuals could both voice their opinions and still stay on the same team.

As we move forward, I hope we can find a way to bridge the gap and accept the word nigga in the Black community without much debate. Frankly, I do not believe you have much choice because it is here to stay just like us. Stay strong My Niggas!

Alleys, Basements, Rooftops, and Staircases

Growing up in urban communities, there is a lot of activity that goes on in alleys, basements, rooftops, and staircases. In some cases, these activities can be illegal or in others, these areas serve as a temporary pit-stop to gather your thoughts, alter or change your clothing, provide a shortcut, offer shelter, or serve as a meeting place for both youth and adults. It is not unusual to see people congregating in one of these areas for some type of purpose. In my lifetime, I have spent time in these areas for both illegal and legal means. In some cases, these areas provide temporary privacy for people who are in public but need to complete a task. I can remember spending time as a teenager with many adults in my neighborhood in one of these areas, usually with the intent to sell them some form of illegal drug. These were not major transactions and usually consisted of marijuana or a small amount of cocaine. Many of the truckers and airport people that would become my regular customers eventually developed a relationship with me, which at times even meant us getting high together. This was not an everyday occurrence, but it happened far more times than you would expect. The fact that I was their supplier gave me credibility as an adult even though I was still a minor. It is a funny thing about drugs that it makes everybody equal. Once you are getting high, morals go out the window. There was one customer that I had that I would always meet in the staircase of his office right on the outskirts of the airport. Usually this would take place on a Friday just after noon. I remember the bills always being fresh because usually he had just come from the bank after cashing his check. We would always discuss sports and from time to time take a one on one from the small bill I kept for my personal. He was very comfortable on the premises of his workplace and never did anyone approach me or venture down that staircase while I was there. He was the perfect customer, and from what I could see he was well respected around the office. Other staff thought I was a messenger, and to be honest in most ways I was. Later his requests would increase, and I figured out that he was supplying others in the office. I understood, like most users, this was his way to get his for free; by buying a larger quantity, he could put a cut on it and then resell the cut version to his clientele. He did this for quite some time, and I was really sorry when he relocated to another state. In our last meeting, we parted as if I was a co-worker.

I had several customers like this and also truckers who needed to stay up for long periods of time. Many of them consume a lot of coffee but nothing gets you as wired as coke. These truckers were my favorites because it was an easy sale, and they were so entertaining with their stories of their travels. Many even traveled with women who wanted to party while the trucker went from state to state on company time.

As I remember my meetings in these places, I wonder what many of these adults really thought of me? Did they respect or like me? Or did any of that matter as long as I came through for them? No adult customer ever uttered to me that you should not be doing this or maybe you need to re-think your life. In fact, many offered advice on how I could increase my sales and get more customers.

When we look at why so many of our youth are confused and make such poor choices in their lives, we must look at the adults who are providing the leadership to them. Too many of the adults provide no direction for our children and then abandon them when they need them most.

The flip side to me is that I also gained trust of many people in some of these meetings in alleys, basements, rooftops, and staircases. These areas offered us privacy when we did not have any other place to go. Many parents made their kids go outside, unlike today where it is the exact opposite with technology providing computers, games, and cell phones with texting and of course social media. Many of my friends and I spent a lot of time in the streets in the '70s and '80s, and if you had to get your own money, you had to know how to dip into an alley or staircase to take care of some business. It was not unusual for you to know what building had faulty doors and alarms that you could jimmy to get to the roof. Staircases always were my favorite because many of my customers worked in buildings and in our day, you didn't have to worry about cameras. Even as a grown man I have always chosen the steps over an elevator. Funny thing my children have also.

As I look back, I strongly believe that we allow our youth to have too much free time. There is an absence of quality youth educational and recreational programs. Many of the organizations that operate these programs are not putting the money allocated into the program. These funds seem to be going in everyone's pockets while our children continue to suffer. We have to increase services to youth and appoint a trusted community liaison to steer those funds to organizations that have the people who can communicate with our children. This liaison will be someone that has already demonstrated his or her commitment to the community. You would be surprised of how many communities have people like this who would step up to the plate. Our communities have to do it from within; there are too many outsiders in Black and Hispanic communities that have jobs and are selling our children out. We need people who view working with children of color as more than a job; that is why our children are suffering.

The other day I went by to see my mother who lives on the ninth floor. When departing, I usually take the steps, and I did so on this occasion. On my way down, I happened to pass a kid from my youth program and his older friend who was totally startled to see me. I said, "what's up" and he acknowledged "what's up G" with a bright smile as we slapped five and hugged. While never missing a beat I said, "stay out of trouble" and he responded, "I will." I believe taking the stairs was something that has come full circle for me. That day it was a reminder to that young man that you never know who you will see at anytime or anywhere and that he needed to rethink how he operated. I am sure that episode impacted his life more than all of his teachers put together. For me, it was a reminder that life has not changed much at all. I will continue to take the stairs; I just hope the quality of people, particularly adults that conduct business on them, get better.

Egg and Cheese

Every morning on my way to school the first thing I would get was an egg & cheese on a roll. One of the first things my mother taught me was to have breakfast. Having breakfast enabled me to think better, and I always have taken great pride in being prepared. I can remember vividly as a little boy standing in line at either Hans or Eddie's Deli with the truckers ordering my egg and cheese. Sometimes some of them would even get a little annoyed because they had to wait for this little Black boy to order. However, at both establishments, they would show me great respect because I was a loyal customer, and they knew me well. Years later, I would work at the local stationary store, and the owners of both stores would all pass through for something, and our relationships grew even stronger.

In my teen years, particularly in junior high and high school, I continued this same habit. I can remember hanging out all night long with Rad in after-hour spots all over the city and then getting my egg and cheese while I walked to school. While Rad took me all over, he still made sure I went to school and would tell me when I fucked up. While I admit it was not the ideal life for a teenager, it made me grow up fast. In my leadership role, I can remember taking Bill, Ben, Junie, Boobs, Sha, Rick, Mice, and others under my wing and schooling them to the best of my ability. For the most part, all of us are still going strong. We have lost some along the way, and some of us are living with some serious issues, but we are surviving.

To emphasize the importance of breakfast in my world, I can remember getting an egg and cheese the morning of an English regent in my senior year of high school. After spending the whole night sniffing coke at Jimbo's spot with Rad and Mac, I raced through the test (I was also flying) because I wanted to finish and get out of there. The funny thing is I did pretty well. The fact that I had breakfast made a big difference in me being able to focus enough to get through. Again, I am not glorifying the use of drugs at any age. In fact, I am trying to send a point to all, never use drugs. Too many young people are being introduced to drugs from people who know little if any about drugs. In my era, there were not as many teens experimenting with drugs and alcohol the way it is now. Yes, there were issues, but now with the addition of cell phones, internet, and social media being drunk, high, and disorderly is a common occurrence.

I guess the point I am trying to make in a very strange way is that even if you find yourself living wrong, try to establish some form of discipline for yourself. In the long run, this may be the only thing that brings you back to a decent life. In my case, I always had breakfast, worked out, and went to school. As a man in his early 20's, this enabled me to walk away from drugs and never look back.

In the Black community, nutrition is something that is not emphasized enough. While there are some free breakfast programs, many still do not eat everyday. Many children and adults are hungry, and this only adds to the poor living conditions that many are faced with already.

For many of my street soldiers, I can only offer some words of advice. As you get up early each morning and venture out, stop by the local bodega and get that egg and cheese. First, you will be putting money back into your hood; secondly you will be preparing yourself for the day, and lastly and more importantly, by feeding your mind, maybe you will be focused enough to make some good decisions. One of those decisions may be to find another way before it is too late.

I know it sounds crazy, but I am a living testimony to how important breakfast is to your life. Let me be clear; there are more nutritional foods out there than an egg and cheese on a roll, and parents, family members, and educators, it is imperative that you ensure that your children start their day off on the right foot. However, for the rest of us, sometimes you have to do what have to do and if that means an egg and cheese on the roll for breakfast then so be it. In some cases, this may be all you get.

By the way, when my money was right, I did slide a little pastrami in there!

Re-Up

When you are on the streets, you are always making decisions.
One of the biggest decisions no matter what you are in to is
whether or not to continue; in other words, will you re-up. When
you re-up, you are replenishing your supply for sale and for
possible profit. Usually when you re-up, it means that your
business is moving enough in the right direction that you had
enough money to get more. The big question is, should you?
There are many people who should never hustle in the streets or
be part of the illegal drug world. It is a vicious world, whether
you are the seller or the user. I have been on both parts of the
seesaw, and I can tell you first-hand it is a roller-coaster at best.

After some of you have gone through the experimental phase of
wanting to be a drug dealer and it is time to re-up, do us all a
favor and don't. Please take that money and do something else.
Time and time again there are people who think the streets are a
playground and they end up dead.

My man and I always went together when we needed to make a
move. We were precise and followed the plan to a tee. When we
went to re-up, we wasted little time with small talk. Our money
was always ready and could be easily counted. We were in and
out and on our way back on schedule almost always. On one
particular occasion while traveling, we were pulled over by an
unmarked car. They did everything in their power to shake us up
while conducting an illegal search of the vehicle. Although we
both were scared as hell, we held our composure and answered
all questions with little hesitation. My man is the type that for the
most part would remain calm; however, if you pushed him too
far, he would get his point across. Well, while one of the officers
was cool, the other just couldn't let go. My man let him know
without raising his voice that they had completed the illegal
search, and it was time for them to move on. It really got under
that officer's skin, and when we pulled off, you could still see
how frustrated he looked. The flip side for us was that we were
lucky that they did not find the stash. Ask any person who has

151

ever been on a pick-up or delivery of a large quantity of illegal drugs, they will tell you it is hell on your nerves. There are times when I think about these travels, and I am amazed how fortunate I was to never spend any major time behind bars. The drug game is a vicious cycle, and there are times when you finally say enough is enough.

In the early '80s, a very close friend of mine who I consider a very experienced street hustler had just completed a major score when he was pulled over for a taillight. The officers were part of a major task force that just wouldn't let go and called in the search dogs, which eventually found the stash. The irony of the situation was that we had just had a conversation about him getting out. He wanted to complete this last score; finish that off and be done. He had already laid the groundwork for opening a business and wanted to have additional capital to keep his life going until his business started earning a profit. It was a good plan, but the chance you take every time you re-up is a huge one. Sometimes you are careless, other times some one has snitched on you, and last but not least your luck just runs out.

I hope that there are some young people who will read this and call it a day. I spent a lot of time in the street as a teen and a grown man, and I can tell you very few make it without doing some time. The odds are just against you to have a long life selling illegal drugs. You may be lucky and make it on your next trip, but when you do, make it the last time you re-up, if not you will be lucky for the wrong reason.

Consignment Package

Credit is a tool that is widely used in our culture. Credit can make your life better or in some cases it can destroy you. It allows you the ability to receive goods and services in lieu of cash with the opportunity to pay at a later date. Usually when you use credit, you have to pay an interest fee for the use of credit. Many people use credit on a daily basis, and without it they probably wouldn't get by. For others, they abuse credit and never catch up. In our society, our worth is determined by a credit score, which many businesses use to determine whether they will extend credit to us. The better your score the better opportunity you have to receive credit. No matter what role you play in life it is important that you pay your debts, failure to do so will only make your life more difficult.

On the streets, many hustlers receive credit in form of what we call a consignment package. A consignment package is where you receive your goods up front without paying anything, and then you pay the supplier once you have sold the goods. While this practice is normal in everyday life, it takes on a different meaning in the street. Many of the hustlers who use this form of credit are probably not disciplined hustlers. They are probably the ones that break all of the rules, including the number one rule, "never get high on your own supply." They are the ones that will probably get someone hurt, including an innocent person. Again, I am not condoning the sale of illegal drugs or any other illegal item; I am dealing with reality in hopes of reaching some people that will understand where I am coming from.

If you are on the streets and in the drug game and are getting your drugs on consignment, you probably will create additional problems for yourself before you make things better. First, you are probably getting high far more than you think. You are to at the point where you have a major problem and things will only get worse. At best you are a functional addict, fiend, junkie, or crackhead. Second, the person or persons you are coping from will eventually grow tired of extending you credit, and you will

153

more than likely still owe them when this happens. Third, you are probably selling an inferior product to your customers because your major goal is to get high and not make money. Last, but not least, you are affecting those around you because your life is a mess, and there are people around you who either are not strong enough or are scared to tell you to get out and get some help. Like any business, success is based on the ability to sell your goods for a profit. In your case, you are always behind. Many of you are fronting wanting others to believe that you are this high-powered drug dealer, but behind the scenes you are severely in trouble. You have a major addiction; you are probably living with somebody that you pay little toward the rent; the car you drive is in your girlfriends name, if you have one, and you are not taking care of your children.

There are so many people like this that are living amongst us. In our community's, drug use is already a major issue. We do not need to compound it with phonies. Again, I am not advocating the sale of illegal drugs, but by dealing with it on a realistic level maybe we can deter some people from remaining in the game. The drug game is a game that can cause you and maybe someone close to you their life. If you are involved and especially if you are getting drugs on consignment, start planning your way out.

I once knew a kid name Mel who was always getting drugs on consignment. Mel was always high and lived with his drug using girlfriend. Mel would always be grandstanding acting like he was on top of the world, but the reality was he was always in the hole. Mel was hustling to get high and that was his only priority. One day some stick-up kids ran up on Mel at his place because they believed he had some money and drugs. To their surprise when they found his stash, there was nothing there. Feeling frustrated they killed both Mel and his girlfriend. Weeks later those same stick-up kids tried to pull this same move on a more experienced hustler, and let's just say they came up empty.

We live in a world where illegal drugs will always be a part of it. Getting drugs on credit is a sign of desperation whether you are the supplier or the user. If you are going to use credit, make sure it is for something you really need. Life is short, and it is something that you never get on consignment!

Fist Fights Vs. Guns

A lot has changed since I was a young boy. The rise in the use of guns has become a major issue in the hood. To many of us, it doesn't even matter if the gun was illegal or legal; the major concern is that things escalated to the point that a gun was involved. The other disturbing factor is that the age for people being involved in the use of guns has become younger and younger. While you will have those in law enforcement that will be quick to use this as ammunition to enforce their gun laws, but to us who know better, again we have to cite the absence of strong men in the hood. We are all fully aware that the system is designed to exploit men of color, but we make it easy for them to exploit us. Many of our young people are so confused to what manhood is that they will pull their guns over some of the most ridiculous things you could imagine. Small disagreements easily turn to heated arguments, which escalate into violence, which ultimately turns into gun play.

In earlier eras, fist fights were very common. Two parties that did not see eye to eye would be quick to settle their differences over a fist fight. These fights could be quick or go on for hours. In most cases, no one else got involved and very few resulted in anyone needing medical assistance. I can remember sitting on the curb and watching some great fights with some dudes that were very good with their hands. Reputations were made and broken over fist fights. Usually in school when two people had differences, they would agree to meet up after school at 3:00 PM in the yard and get it on. I still remember the signs for the fight, which included someone punching their hands and holding up three fingers and then pointing to the person you would fight. The great thing about these encounters was that rarely did anyone jump in. Both parties fought until someone gave up or was clearly beaten. In those days the only embarrassment was not fighting. Losing was accepted as long as you fought, and people rarely lost respect for you if you put up a decent effort. The great thing about these fights was that after the fight was over that was the end of it. It was not rare to see both parties hanging out the next day. I am not condoning this activity today because the mindset is different; then, adults understood this as well. It was not uncommon for them to allow two people to fight under the condition that after the fight was over that was the end of it. In the seventh grade, one of my teachers Mr. Nance, a very cool motherfucker, allowed two of my friends to fight right in the class. He got tired of them bickering and called their bluff. He told me to post a piece of construction paper over glass on the door; he then had some other classmates move the desks and chairs out of the way and let them get it on. They fought for about five minutes without anyone really being declared the winner. He swore the class to secrecy, and we all stuck to it. No one ever got out of hand in Mr. Nance's class again after that. They knew he was a real man not a just a teacher that would call your bluff. After that incident, our class seemed to grow closer; the fact that we carried that secret made our bond stronger. I remember at the teacher's talent show all of the students gave Mr. Nance a standing ovation; he deserved it for his performance, but you have to wonder what other lessons he had taught his students. In another incident, my wife always talks about the time her father made her fight a neighbor on her block. The children of the two families had been beefing for some time when things got out of hand. One of the female children from the other family was really becoming disrespectful in front of the house, and Pop (her father) was becoming frustrated. Keep in mind he is a very private and proud person but could not take it anymore. After listening to her continue to mouth off, he shouted, "Toni get out their and kick her ass!" After several altercations that day, the families eventually came to a truce and remain good friends until today. Pop understood that they needed to bring the situation to an end, if he allowed it to fester who knows what could have happened.

Today the mindset is so different, and it isn't rare to see people walk around with guns on a regular basis. Going to school, work, or hanging on the corner some young people are holding. Has life changed that much that you need your gun on a regular basis? How many of you are putting yourself in the position that you will have to use that gun simply because you have it and your peers are around? A rule I lived by my entire life is that if you need to bring a gun to your destination, then you probably should not go. That rule will always make sense. Secondly, that gun should be in a spot that requires you to think twice before you actually pull it out. Third, before you actually leave with that gun, you have already determined there is a strong chance your life is over.

Many of you will ignore my warnings because you believe you are so much of a thug that you need your gun at all times. Maybe you are right, but at the end of the day, your life will either be terminated by another thug, the police, an innocent party, or maybe even yourself. A lot of you are fronting anyway. Some of you are walking around with a gun with no intention of ever using it. How smart is that? Plaxico Burress is guilty of that. I like Plax and from what I have heard, he is a cool dude, but what was he thinking? He is a 6'6 professional football star; was he really going to pull his gun and shoot somebody in the club? Tory Lanz is also guilty of the same thing. Some of you are in the same boat as them and have no intention of using that gun, so do us all a favor and get rid of it. Please change your life before it is too late.

Maybe one day things will revert back to the old days when people actually fought in the streets with no weapons involved. I welcome that with open arms. We all know there will be disagreements, but maybe just maybe when the fight is over, we can all have a drink.

Wakes and Funerals

One thing that I can tell you as I begin to write this chapter is that at 60 years old, I am done going to wakes and funerals for young people killed in the street. I have used up my chances. I have been to so many wakes and funerals for young people that have been killed in the street that I cannot take it anymore. In most of these cases, guns were involved and someone was killed. In most of the cases, one of the parties involved was somehow involved in street activity. In most of these cases, the tragedy could have been avoided if all parties involved took a little time to weigh the consequences. In most of these cases, peer pressure played a role in the decision to go all the way. Too many of our young people devalue life, and I strongly believe it is getting worse.

Going to wakes and funerals for some of these young people that have been killed as a result of the streets has become too comfortable. People show up at these events like it is a social event and do not understand the significance of what is at stake. They show up inappropriately dressed and do not posses the proper etiquette that is associated respecting the loss of a life. What I have witnessed I am really ashamed of, including people congregating and talking on their cell phones as if they are at a club. Many are loud and cannot remain in their seats. The constant movement and the need to go in and out of the building feeding their desire to answer or make irrelevant calls. Many people attend high as a kite. Again, take note world although times are hard for many, it is imperative that if you can own several pairs of footwear that one should be a pair of shoes (black). You cannot call yourself a man and not own a pair of shoes. I have been around some official goons in my life, and they knew how to dress for these events. So, to a goon from a goblin get some shoes. Women the tight clothes and short outfits are not appropriate dress for a wake or funeral. Let the audience spend their time honoring the deceased and not your ass!

At the last wake I attended, I witnessed some of the poorest behavior possible. Things got heated and a fight resulted. Enough is enough!

As a people, we have to improve on our quality of life. How we manage death is a firm testimonial on how we live. When you decide to attend a wake or funeral, go properly prepared to embrace and celebrate the life of the deceased. Understand that his family and friends need your support and love at this very tough time. Seeing you properly dressed, sober, fresh, and articulate will only bring positive energy to the event, the family, friends, and other guests.

In all of my years around my friends and colleagues that are Caucasian, it was extremely rare for me to hear them speak of attending a wake or funeral for young person killed as a result of violence in the street. At worse, it would be a driving incident that could have involved alcohol. That says a lot about how we view life and death. We have to do a better job of educating our children about living a full life that includes achieving goals. Wakes and funerals involving young people killed as a result of street violence have to become a rare incident. We need our young people to have quality adolescence, teen years, and adulthood. Life must be valued at all cost. The only way possible to achieve this lofty goal is to make our children feel good about themselves each day. Quality adults can raise quality children. Parents, grandparents, relatives, educators, and other adults need to get their lives in order, so that they can guide and lead the children. The fact that many of the adults have dropped the ball has led to this acceptance of young death. Everyone who considers themselves an adult must assume some role of assisting with the children they come in contact with. The smallest contribution matters.

The old saying, "It takes a Village to Raise a Child," is more relevant today than ever before. Stop hiding and being afraid of our children. Many people today say these children today are out of control. I disagree. I think the adults are the ones that are crazy. How else can you explain paying all of the bills and being disrespected in your own home as parents!

9 to 5 vs. Entrepreneur

There are both similarities and differences in working a 9 to 5 and being an entrepreneur. Both are challenging and both can take years off of your life. Pressure is a part of both and being responsible can make the difference in how far you go in your career. A 9 to 5 builds a sense of stability because you usually are guaranteed a salary, healthcare, life insurance, and possibly a pension. You typically know how much money the 9 to 5 will generate, and your schedule is planned because you have either scheduled or confirmed vacation for the year. Unless you are the head of the company, you report to somebody. If you have a great relationship with that person life can be pleasant; if you don't, then life can be hell. In my experiences working a 9 to 5, I never really had any issues with some of the people that I reported to. I was always responsible and performed well. In fact, I learned some things from some of the people I reported to. My problem with most of them was their ability to deal with people. They really had no clue about people. I think this is the problem with corporate America. They really don't understand people. The most important asset for any company is your ability to communicate your message. If people can get the message, they can deliver the product. I can call any young person (there have been many) that has worked for me, and I will guarantee they will say nothing but positive things about their experiences working with me. I get calls and emails from my people checking in and letting me know how they are doing all of the time. We built trust, and people understood that they needed to be responsible and complete their duties each day. My people could tell me the truth and understood that my decisions would be based on common sense and not dictated by company policy, which at times made no sense. People with children were treated differently than those who didn't have any. If one person made a poor decision, sometimes everyone paid for it. I cursed at some of my staff, and there were others that I never raised my voice to. Everyone was different. Sometimes I shared things with my staff that I may have been told to keep to my self from my directors or executives. Fuck you on that one; these were my people, and they were ride or die for me and me for them.

Working 9 to 5s are good places to learn business and develop a strong work ethic. Discipline is very important, and, in most cases, you will have to assimilate in order to elevate the corporate ladder. Your ability to switch channels (hood, corporate, leisure) will be very important to your survival, because you never want to continue to be the only Black person at a convention, class, or event. Give yourself a plan that clearly states how many years you will put into corporate America. My plan was to work in corporate America for twenty-five years and that is what I did. Your talents and energy will be consumed while working a 9 to 5. If your desire one day is to start your own business, then you need to store some of your talents and energy for when you are ready to make your move. Don't get me wrong; while you are there, work your butt off, but know in your head that you have a plan. Seek out professional people that can guide and mentor you as you move forward. Develop a business plan and start to develop a financial strategy that will enable you to live and carry out your plan. It will be tough, but you can do it.

I have operated my own non-profit organization for thirty-six years. In that time, we have serviced thousands and brought resources, including jobs and programs to many in New York City. In addition, I have worked for other corporations in decision making positions and still believe that most managers, directors, and hierarchy have no idea how to manage people.

I have been an entrepreneur as well my entire life, but that role was really elevated after I left corporate America. Being an entrepreneur is the hardest thing that most will ever encounter. The bottom line is the buck stops with you. You wear a thousand hats, which basically means you do it all. Many don't understand that when they put the entrepreneur hat on that you have to get it all done each day. The growth of your business is directly affected by how much you put into the business.

163

I have partnered on a couple of projects with my wife, and they have been the best decisions I have ever made. I am in a rare position because my wife's work ethic may be stronger than mine, but I may not be ready to admit that yet. But that is a win either way. We have shared so much together, and at this point in our lives to be working together is a testimonial to our marriage. At times we may have a small disagreement, but it never lasts long. A strong marriage is the ability to say, "fuck you" and be alright later on. We are both mature enough to move on because we understand the big picture. We are attempting to build businesses in a tough economic climate and must stay focused to survive.

There is a lot of pressure being an entrepreneur, but Blacks and other people of color must begin again to build our own businesses that can compete with anybody. Too many of our children are being educated and trained to work for someone else. Parents must make the entrepreneurial road as part of the education for their children at an early age. In the '50s and '60s, we owned businesses and built communities. We need to get that back to that with a young movement advocating young business owners with financial packages from the government that speaks of helping all people.

Lastly, people of color need to stop hating on each other and patronize small businesses. You are only hurting yourself when you discriminate against small businesses owned by people of color. Others will respect you more when they see small businesses in your communities growing and displaying pride in their products and services. On the flip side, people of color who own small businesses must have their shit together to attract customers.

Whatever your choice, be a responsible adult and develop a plan!

Car Notes

Cars play too big of a role in our communities. We have so many of our people in bad financial situations simply because they chose to either buy or lease a car that they could not afford. Even worse, many of them are not even the ones who are driving the car. How many people in our communities have put a car in their name for someone else? The answer is too many. If someone comes to you and asks you to put car in your name, a red flag should go up. There should be few if any circumstances when you should use your credit for someone else. People who have abused their credit will eventually abuse yours. People who didn't pay their bills will continue not to pay their bills. Don't be fooled because they get off on the right foot; sooner or later their true colors will show, and you will be getting a call from the dealer informing you that the payments have not been made. Women are extremely vulnerable to this fiasco of using their credit to keep a man in their life. It is bad enough that they do it for cell phones, but many graduates to car notes. Most of you have been raised better, and those who haven't should merely use common sense. You are being used, and when the relationship ends, you will have to pay the price for your poor decision.

Many men in the hood strongly believe that driving a luxury car will elevate their status. Yes, they will fool a lot of people, mostly dick riders and women of low esteem. It is not uncommon for us to see an attractive woman jumping out of a luxury car of a person we know; this was not the case before he was driving this car. It is not uncommon for us to see a bunch of dudes driving around the hood going nowhere in a luxury car just wanting to be seen. In fact, many people in the hood are identified by what they are driving. This is the attraction of luxury cars in the hood. They turn nobodies into some bodies, at least they think so.

How many times have we witnessed somebody from the hood who has received some kind of settlement, and what is the first thing they purchase? A car! Why? A car gives them a false sense of purpose, a feeling of power. They attract women or men and

165

new friends. They can go places they never went before and now can be identified more easily.

The sad part for many of these people is that not much else changes. Many even remain in poor living conditions; sleep in the same old bed, and use the same towels and linen that need replacing. Common sense would say get a decent car and improve the more important aspects of your lives, including your home and personal effects. Instead, you would rather impress strangers and continue to dry your body with a towel with a hole in it. Instead of calling a plumber to fix that leak that you have been using that bucket for the last year, you get new rims. It is really sad how important cars are to us. Don't get me wrong, if you can afford it and your shit is together, more power to you. Just be aware that once you drive that car off of the lot, it depreciates (loses value) immediately. So, make wise decisions on how much money you will put into a car. We have too many people hiding cars in garages and parking lots so they will not be repossessed by the dealer because they got in way over their heads.

Many men even put cars before their families and especially their children. It is not uncommon for a man to pay his car note before his child support. It is not uncommon for a man to pay his car note before he gives his mother money for rent, even though he is still staying there. It is not uncommon for a man to get a woman to pay his car note and never let her drive the car. I single men out because they are the main culprits and they know it. There are some women who play this game as well, but it is mostly a male addiction.

Even today there is a segment of our population who rent luxury cars at appalling rates just so they can floss and be seen in the hood and at specialty events. These same fools will also run a tab on bottle service and probably pay with a fraudulent credit card. Sound familiar?

Again, cars are much too important to us. Others races and cultures seem to put less emphasis on cars and more on education, building businesses, and developing their children. WE can learn a thing or two from people who would drive a hoop die (old car), get a solid education, develop a plan, and start a family when they are ready. I know I will have detractors on this that will say that who am I to say when to start a family. My answer to you is that if we begin to teach our young to family plan and that is a part of their education, we will reduce the amount of single-parent families that exist in abundance in our communities. Anyone who would argue with that is a fool and to be quite frank probably an asshole too!

The reality is that a car will not make you a better person or increase the likelihood that you will have a successful life. It is a mirage that will eventually evaporate, and then you will wake-up and see your car on flatbed because you failed to pay your car note!

Looking Fly

Nothing is more important in the hood than looking fly. In other words, emphasizing hair, clothes, and shoes. So many of our people are more concerned with how they look than anything else. I will admit that in my life I have spent money on my share of Gucci, Prada, Louie, and many others. In looking back on my life, I have always been a slave to fashion. My entire family, including my wife and children, have also fell victim to this disease. I call it a disease because it is equal to alcoholism, drug addition, and gambling. As adults, we are guilty of setting up our children to want to look a certain way. This, later on in life, leads them to do things we would not approve of, including selling drugs, committing robbery, stripping, and using fraudulent credit cards to name a few.

Take a trip down the main streets of any urban Black community and two of the main businesses that you will see will be hair salons and barbershops. It is kind of a catch 22 in the hood because these small businesses are important to our communities and provide income for many of our residents. The flip side is that many of the customers value how their hair looks over other elements of their lives that should take priority over their hair. Let me be clear; I am not trying to take money out of the hands of these businesses; I am merely stating that we must become more fiscally responsible and be able to take care of our bills, feed our children, and then be savvy enough to maintain our appearance. You cannot get your hair done before you pay the electric bill. That makes no sense. You cannot get a haircut and your kids are hungry. That makes no sense. We have not done a great job of managing our priorities over the years, and it has been a major factor in the Black community remaining in the poor condition.

So many of our people today are walking around in European designer (Prada, Gucci, Louie Vuitton) clothes with no direction. Once something catches on in the hood, everyone must have it. Many will do whatever is necessary to achieve the "Ghetto Fabulous" label. Many will wonder why? But it is very simple.

Everyone desires to be wanted and being fly in the hood will make you wanted. It elevates your status, and believe it or not it makes many feel good about themselves. It is short lived because at the end of the day your status has not changed because of the way you look. Clothes enhance who you are; they do not elevate your status in life. Many of us need to look at who we are and try and establish a "Life Plan" that will ensure that we set and meet goals (financial and others), become somewhat educated, take care of our children and elderly, empower our communities, and do more good than bad. If along the way you want to look good doing it, that is fine, but other factors must replace the ones we currently embrace.

Again, I admit to being a part of this problem, but at the same time I also have taken care of my responsibilities throughout my life. I love clothes and have always been ahead of most in the arena of fashion. I take great pride in how I look, and over the years I have learned that less is more. When I turned fifty years old ten years ago, I gave half of my clothes to many people who I thought could use them more than me. Many were surprised that I was giving away clothes that still fit me that looked practically new. My rationale was that others could benefit more, and to be perfectly honest I just wanted to start a new chapter in my life. I kept the clothes that were special to me and others that would be hard to replace. My wife did the same thing, and we noticed after that period we both still had more than enough in our respective wardrobes. We wanted to grow as people, and sometimes in life you have to lighten the load in order for other things to come into your life.

Moving forward, I will do my best to influence my grandchildren to appreciate fashion without becoming a slave to it. Once you are hooked, it is hard to shake like any other addiction. In my daily travels, I still continue to see babies dressed in designer clothing with teenage parents and clueless grandparents who have no idea of the monsters they are creating. I will continue to see Gucci belts below the waist wondering where do these young people keep their wallets (if they have one)? I will continue to see women with designer bags both real and fake who have no money in them or a credit card they can use. I will continue to see styles change and people change with the styles even though in most cases they cannot afford the change.

Our people have been victimized by a system that has held us down since slavery. We all understand this by now and most of us look for something to make us feel good because life is a bitch sometimes. We must change our priorities for the sake of our children. If not, we will continue to raise children that will value how they look over what they think.

I have made a pledge to myself that I will practice what I preach. I have done that over the last ten years, focusing less on fashion and more on achieving the lofty goals I have set for myself. I will put my resources into my family and the many children and adults that view me as a leader. I hope many of the adults in the hood will follow this example, especially those that have limited resources. We cannot blame our children for finding a way to feel good about themselves when we have done a horrible job of doing it ourselves. Many parents need to put less money into material goods and more into spending quality time with their children. We can change the mind set of our people with a lot of work and commitment. Otherwise other cultures will continue to laugh at Blacks wearing expensive clothing that in most cases they could not afford. The choice is ours.

By the way, some of you are looking real fly lately!

Life is a Business

Contrary to what many believe, there is no real difference between business and personal. Your life is a business, and you should treat it as such. You should have rules, procedures, and policies for your personal life. There should be things you rarely do and things that you would never consider. You should have discipline and punish yourself when you know in your heart that you have done wrong. For instance, if you spent money on a vice or are out of character in front of strangers, you should punish yourself for those transgressions. As an adult, you should not wait for others to dole out a punishment to you. Particularly with employment (jobs), many of you allow the people you work for to decide how well you are doing in life and decide when you should be punished. Corporate America is designed in this manner. Many people damn near kill themselves to prove to supervisors and managers that they are performing well when many of these managers and supervisors don't have their shit together. How can a person whose shit is not together evaluate you? Some people would say it is two different situations. I totally disagree. No one knows you better than you know yourself. You know when you are performing well, and you know when you are performing poorly. Common sense says that when your shit is together all around the board, then you are in a position to evaluate me. On the flip side, when some of you get a good evaluation at work, then you deem in your mind that you are living well. While that may be part of the equation, there are so many other things in life you must be excelling at to be evaluated as doing well. Do you take good care of your children? Are the elderly people (mother, father, aunts, uncles) in your life well cared for? Are you paying your bills on time? Are you excising and take care of your body? Are you in a healthy relationship?

There are so many factors that go into running your life that you must remain focused at all times. There will be times, no matter how good a person you are, that you will drift outside of your good character. These times should come few and far between as you get older. I have met some really good people who have addictions, including drugs, alcohol, gambling, and some others (not necessary to mention). Some of these people are very responsible, and although they dip and dab, they still manage to get things done in life. I thought I would mention *you* because we need to be honest in the hood and say, do your thing but take care of your business.

I had a friend who had a great job and a cocaine chippy at the same time, which could be a very dangerous combination. A chippy is when you like cocaine, a habit is when you love cocaine. If you are not careful, a chippy can easily turn into a habit. He worked his ass off, but when he felt the urge, he would cop and do his thing. Over the years, his usage decreased to the point where he would only use on holidays and his birthday. This is an example of great discipline in dealing with a realistic situation. People will continue to get high, but we must have self-discipline for us to turn the Black community around. You must begin to get your addictions under control before you can move forward. I understand that, in some cases, we are dealing with both mental and physical health issues, but we don't have time in our current position to wait. Business requires discipline. Life requires discipline. If you haven't already, start associating life with business and business with life.

Another issue that must be addressed is being on time. Black people should always be early. I will not mention the acronym that goes with the Black community because, to me, it is very insulting that it exists. Again, I reiterate, Black people should always be early.

It is time for us to take responsibility for uplifting our community. It starts with that look in the mirror. Is your life in order? Are your important papers properly stored in a file cabinet for easy viewing or stashed away in a paper bag? Are your bills being paid, and are you maintaining the proper records to confirm payments, or are you always late and incurring late charges? Do you schedule appointments, including your personal tasks, and tend to stay on schedule, or are you late everywhere? Are you taking care of your body and mind, or is your behavior reckless? How are the relationships in your life? Relationships are a big part of who we are. These relationships can include husband and wife, boyfriend and girlfriend, mother and daughter, or even grandmother and grandson. There are so many combinations to this scenario. How you manage these relationships will dictate how your life goes. Some of the time for these relationships should be scheduled, some not, but give thought in how you handle each. Even leaving a note for yourself sometimes to give someone a call can mean a lot at the right time.

Nothing matters more than people. I do my best to always put people first. I have taught my children to always put people first. I believe they get it now, but I know sometimes they would get annoyed when they were younger. Don't get me wrong. They knew better than to say too much.

As we move forward in our communities, we must make an effort to keep them cleaner and in better overall condition. Little things like picking up garbage in the street and putting our shopping carts back at the supermarket say a lot about how we live. Even those of you who get high, why do you leave your evidence in the street? In my day, you would conceal your paraphernalia and discard the evidence at the proper time. Now, so many of you drop your blunt shavings and wrappers right in the very spot you are getting high. What sense does that make? Where is your discretion?

Personally, I have always tried to meet high expectations for myself. I keep a weekly schedule, work-out consistently, spend time with my family and meet my financial obligations. There have been times when I have ventured outside of this regimen, but I have always found myself back. I am extremely neat and organized, so it is not a difficult task for me. However, my greatest attribute, I believe, is that I hold myself personally accountable for my actions. I will not hesitate to punish myself. I have gone so far as to not eat lunch on a day at work because I missed a belt loop on my pants. To me, this is important because it is attention to detail, and while no one else knew—I did. I hope some of you are getting it. Be your biggest critic, and if you are, you will be your biggest fan.

Life is a business no matter what type of life you are leading. If you would like one day to have a great one, you must treat your life as a business. Last, just because it is business doesn't mean you can't have fun!

To-Do List

Each day, I have a to-do list for myself. Sometimes, this list is long, sometimes it is short. It contains both business and personal tasks and can be a combination of both. When you assume the title of adult, you should have daily tasks to keep your life on track and to get your life on track if need be. I have had a to-do list when I was in the street and when I led a rather conservative life. It shouldn't matter what type of life you lead. You should have a busy schedule. It is alarming to me, in this day and time in the Black and Hispanic communities, how so many of you think you have nothing to do. I see so many adults doing nothing each day, waiting for someone to give them direction. There are times in your life when you have to take the bull by the horns and muster the courage to make changes in your life. Sometimes, you will fail, but you will learn from your mistakes. Other times, you will succeed, and this will give you the confidence to take additional risks.

Start off by getting a calendar and putting in tasks for the week. Even if the tasks are minimal, they should be scheduled. This includes chores such as laundry, picking up your clothes from the cleaners, food shopping, and medical appointments. You will find that the more your life is scheduled, the more progress you will make. Some of you should even schedule time with your children because, at times, we forget how important this is. For most of my adult life, I have dedicated my life to the communities I come from. Each week, I have designated periods that I operate my educational and recreational activities for my people. This is important to me because people look for me for direction. They know at certain times of the week, "G" will be in the school, and they can catch me for a one on one conversation that may provide some direction for them. Sometimes, I can provide direction immediately. Other times, I will direct them to the source, or I will get back to them at a later date. Again, it is important for Black men to make themselves available for young Black boys on a regular basis to ensure they get the proper direction. This goes back to having a to-do list, which should have one of the following as its items, work with youth, coach game, practice for baseball team, mentoring session for youth, follow-up on jobs for community, pick-up uniforms, take the team to movies, visit prison, take clothes to shelter, and obtain condoms for participants. If items such as this are part of your list, then you are on the right track. If not, you really need to look in the mirror and reconsider how you are living.

For over thirty years, I have been the easiest person on earth to kill. I say this because anybody who knows me knows that on any Sunday morning, I will be in the gym working with my Fatherhood Program at 8:00 AM no matter what the weather conditions may be if I am in New York City. In fact, I have cut some business trips short, so I could be available on Sunday mornings. First of all, I enjoy spending time with my people, and second, I understand the importance of being there.

My discipline and strength were derived from many of the street hustlers and businessmen I watched as a young boy. I can remember seeing many of them open up their spots at scheduled times each day and having designated times they would bag up and have their products ready for sale. I would incorporate this into my life, emulating them both in my time in the street and later on as an adult working in corporate America. While I am not condoning street activity or crime, I have to be honest and say that the street hustlers were more disciplined in some ways than the people I viewed in the corporate sector. The hustlers had no one managing their time, and there were no policies and procedures manuals for them to follow. They had to set their own rules and be disciplined enough to follow them.

Young hustlers hear me clearly; part of your to-do list every day should contain the words "Last day for my hustle." Please start preparing to get out before it is too late. I had a date for myself in my mid-twenties, and I stuck to it. I know it is easier said than done, but you can do it. Those same skills you have obtained, including budgeting money so you can re-up, packaging drugs, marketing them, selling them, buying and selling merchandise using illegal methods, can be used in a legal setting. It will not happen overnight, but if you start now, you will find your way. I will keep it real with you. Even if you do both until you can get out altogether, that will be a step in the right direction, but that time must be short. Again, I am not advocating crime, but I also must let my street soldiers know there is hope for them.

Technology has provided so many resources for us to get our lives together. Facebook, Instagram, Twitter, Google, iPhones, and other media make it so easy for us to have a daily to-do list at our disposal. Too many of you are not taking advantage of the technology that has been afforded to you. Instead of posting bullshit to your "social media" account, how about spending that time on daily tasks on your to-do list that could assist a family member, friend, or a kid who needs your assistance.

I am very proud of what I have accomplished in my life, but at sixty years old, I still have so much more to do. My to-do list today contains items such as working on a proposal, spending time with my grandkids, talking to my daughter about her career, updating our website, and painting a chair. As you can see, it contains both personal and business items, and yours should as well. Remember, people, especially children, always come first, and while you are at it, make sure you schedule some time for your significant other.

Lying to Yourself

Too many men and women lie to themselves consistently. Men usually lie about their self-worth, and women usually lie about their relationships. As you get older, this practice should happen less and less, but depending on the individual, that is not always the case. Throughout my life, I have seen so many variations, and it usually means that these people never reach their full potential in life.

Your biggest chance at leading a quality life will start when you are honest with yourself. This should not be difficult because only you know what is really going on in your life. You know if you are financially responsible if you are being a responsible parent, taking care of your mind and body, and, most importantly, presenting your true self to others. So many men are living a lie. They present themselves to women driving someone else's car, wearing someone else's clothes, and lying about where they live. These sorry motherfuckers even start to believe that they are this person because many women buy into this false identity because they believe they are in need of a man. I know this will get many feminists up in arms, but the truth is the truth. These men usually are unemployed and are not even decent hustlers. Their craft is lying, and they usually make it by exploiting women. Many of these women make it easy because in their desire for company, they look the other way, and these men know when they have a live one.

Many women have been raised in a home without a father or male role model, so they have no measuring stick of what a true man should be. They are attracted to physical features and a gift of gab, which comes easy to these pieces of shit men with no shame in their game. I was raised by several hustlers who took pride in getting their own money without living off of women. In fact, many helped to take care of several women, because to them, that is what a man should do. I am not defending this practice, but I will gladly take it over the swindlers that have become too common in our communities today.

Men, be on guard of women who want to get a baby out of you so they can get child support. It is a shame we have to bring this to the table, but it is what it is. Many of these women target athletes and entertainers but will settle for a man with a good job. These women have fixed in their minds that this is a legitimate hustle, and it has been co-signed by older family members, including their mothers, aunts, and older sisters. Many of these women spend their whole lives deceiving men, including spending their last at the salon and even getting surgeries on their bodies so they can guarantee some form of payment coming in. The sad part is that many of them will end up all by themselves anyway because you cannot buy character.

Technology has also paid a major role in people lying to themselves. Social media, including Facebook, Instagram, Twitter, and others, have many people clearly misrepresenting who they really are. I have seen some of you posting information that is clearly an attempt to bolster your image. Recently, someone I went to high school with posted an image of himself that was clearly bullshit. This person had done nothing he said he accomplished but had no problems posting lies.

Another major issue is that people are not being honest about their sexuality. Both men and women are in relationships with people who are of a different sexual orientation than you have been led to believe. Men are posing as women and women as men. Others are bisexuals but do not reveal that to potential partners. Many of you may not find this out until you reach the alter, if then, and it will be devastating to your life when you do. Practice due diligence and make it your business to find out who you are in a relationship with. Don't wait for someone to make a fool of you. We are living in a very modern, self-worth world, and LGBTQ people are a part of that world. Discriminating against someone for their lifestyle is bullshit. People should be treated with respect, and quite frankly, what do you care? Mind your business and grow as a person.

People, wake up and take the time to perform self-inventory on yourself. Know what your strong points are and what you need to work on. If you put the effort into both your mind and body, you will become a quality person that others will notice. Have high expectations for yourself and others, and know that nothing is more important than what you think of yourself.

Only cowards continue to lie to themselves because they do not want to face the truth. Each day, ask yourself: Are you in the "winners" or "losers" column at this point in your life? This will dictate how you move and whether you need to make minor or major changes. Many of you are scared to ask the question because you do not want to deal with reality. Instead, you will lie to yourself!

My Library

Over the years, I have compiled a "library" for my family. This collection of books is much diversified, and to the surprise of many, will contain publications that many will be surprised that I read after reading this book. All of these publications have shaped my views over my entire life. My brother, Curtis, is a passionate reader, and I admire his devotion to reading. While I have always preferred to read non-fiction, there have been times in my life where I had no choice but to read the fiction publications that were assigned to me. Unlike many men, I have never been a part of the video game craze and elect to spend my time reading or doing some form of research. In my late teens, my affinity to "Black nationalism" served as the incubator for my thirst for knowledge concerning people of color, particularly Black or African. This would eventually lead to my extended research in the area of Pan-Africanism and authors such as John Hendrik Clarke, Walter Rodney, Ivan Van Sertima, Fantz Fanon, and others. The "Autobiography of Malcolm X" was the most important book of my life; it is the one book that I identified with most. I strongly urge all Black youth, particularly males, to read it at some point in your childhood.

I can remember my grade school days when I worked with the school librarian, Ms. Vander Woolf, where I developed reading skills and became very familiar with the Dewey decimal system. I would restock books and learn to use microfilm. I would also read the works of William Shakespeare, John Steinbeck, Tennessee Williams, and other well-respected authors. I still admire these authors and respect their work but believe that we should have been introduced to Black authors at a much younger age. While I have great admiration for the authors noted above, I did not find them superior to Baldwin, Wright, Hughes, and other great Black authors. The educational system deliberately kept these authors away from us and always put the publications of White authors in front of us as assigned reading. I am certain that many Black youths would become better readers if the materials assigned to them were more related to their own lives. I know, for me, when I started to read Black literature, it changed my life and gave me more confidence in being Black in America.

I think it is every family's duty to establish a library for their children. In some cases, conventional books have given way to e-book readers, such as the Kindle. I maintain that there should always be a place for a library in every home. In the Black community, where we waste resources on other unnecessary items, raising the educational consciousness of our children should be a priority.

Below, you will find a list of some of the books that are part of our library. Please note that this is my own personal taste. While I believe that there are some books below that should be read by young Black America, I will leave that to you to decide. I have always encouraged my children to read, and in the early years, even required book reports from them. While some of the titles may raise some eyebrows, please understand that you should determine what books interest you and make a solid effort to read and store them for future generations. Your life experiences and desire for knowledge will guide building your library. If you allow others to fully dictate the reading material of your children, then they will control their minds and continue the confusion we have witnessed for centuries. Please remember that reading is fundamental.

Selected Publications of the Clifton Library

Book Title	Author(s)
The Autobiography of Malcolm X	Alex Haley
Malcolm X Man and His Times	John Hendrik Clarke
Malcolm – The Life of a Man Who Changed Black America	Bruce Perry
Malcolm X – The Last Speeches	Edited by Bruce Perry
Malcolm X – In Our Own Image	Joe Wood, Editor
Message to the Blackman in America	Elijah Muhammad
An Original Man – The Life and Times of Elijah Muhammad	Claude Andrew Clegg III
Growing Up X	Ilyasah Shabazz
The Days of Martin Luther King Jr.	Jim Bishop
A Testament of Hope: The Essential Writings and Speeches of Martin Luther King Jr.	James Melvin
Let Nobody Turn Us Around an American Anthology	Manning Marable, Leith Mullings
Roots	Alex Haley
Che Guevara – A Revolutionary Life	Jon Lee Anderson
Che: The Diaries of Ernesto Che Guevara	Ocean Press
Africa Must Unite	Kwame Nkrumah
W.E.B. Dubois – Biography of Race	David Levering Lewis
Souls of Black Folks	W.E.B. Dubois
Undiscovered Paul Robeson, an Artists Journey 1898-1939	Paul Robeson Jr.
Afrocentricity	Molefi Asante
How Europe Underdeveloped Africa	Walter Rodney
Groundings with My Brothers, 1st Edition	Walter Rodney
Africans at the Crossroads: Notes for an African World Revolution	John Henrik Clarke
Wrenched of the Earth	Frantz Fanon
Black Skin White Masks	Frantz Fanon
Toward the African Revolution	Frantz Fanon

Book Title	Author(s)
Frank – The Voice	James Kaplan
Mozart a Cultural Biography	Robert W. Gutman
Beethoven: The Music and Life	Lewis Lockwood
Clemente, The Passion and Grace of Baseball's Last Hero	David Maraniss
Long Walk to Freedom – The Autobiography of Nelson Mandela	Little Brown
The Measure of a Man – A Spiritual Autobiography	Sidney Poitier
Before the Legend – The Rise of Bob Marley	Christopher John Farley
Assata – An Autobiography	Assasta Shakur
This Side of Glory – The Autobiography of David Hilliard and the Story of the Black Panther Party	David Hilliard & Lewis Cole
The Shadow of the Panther – Huey Newton and the Price of the Black Power in America	Hugh Pearson
A Taste of Power – A Black Woman's Story	Elaine Brown
Soledad Brother – The Prison Letters of George Jackson	George L. Jackson
Blood in My Eye	George L. Jackson
Nat Turner – Before the Bar of Judgment	Mary Kemp Davis
100 Years of Lynching's	Ralph Ginzburg
All God's Children – The Bosket Family and the American Tradition of Violence	Fox Butterfield
Makes Me Wanna Holler – A Young Black Man in America	Nathan McCall
The Art of War	Sun Tzu
Fatherhood	Bill Cosby

Book Title	Author(s)
The Cornell West Reader	Cornell West
The Falsification of Afrikan Consciousness	Amos Wilson
They Came Before Columbus	Ivan Van Sertima
The Miseducation of the Negro	Carter G. Woodson
Countering the Conspiracy to Destroy Black Boys Volumes I, II, III	Jawanza Kunjufu
Developing Positive Self-Images & Discipline in Black Children	Jawanza Kunjuf
Young Gifted and Black – Promoting High Achievement Among African American Students	Perry/Steele/Hilliard
Reflections of an Urban High School Principal	Bernard Gassaway
My Way – The Leadership Style of an Urban High School Principal	Frank N. Mickens
The Isis Papers	France Cress Welsing
Out of Bounds	Jim Brown with Steve Delsohn
Miles – The Autobiography	Miles Davis with Quincy Troupe
Divided Soul – The Life of Marvin Gaye	David Ritz
Decoded	Shawn Carter
Midnight a Gangster Love Story	Sister Souljah
The Coldest Winter Ever	Sister Souljah
The Collected Poems of Langston Hughes	Langston Hughes
The Ways of White Folk	Langston Hughes
The Big Sea	Langston Hughes
"My People"	Langston Hughes

Book Titles	Author(s)
Our Endangered Values, America's Moral Crisis	Jimmy Carter
Richard M. Nixon: A Life in Full	Conrad Black
Abuse of Power: The New Nixon Tapes	Stanley Kutler
Leaders	Richard M. Nixon
My Life	Bill Clinton
An Unfinished Life – John F. Kennedy 1917-1963	Robert Dallek
JFK: Day by Day: A Chronicle of the 1,036 Days of John F. Kennedy's Presidency	Terry Golway & Les Krantz
Jack Kennedy: Elusive Hero	Christopher Mathews
Team of Rivals – The Political Genius of Abraham Lincoln	Doris Kearns Goodwin
Abraham Lincoln	James McPherson
Lincoln	David Herbert Donald
Living History	Hillary Rodham Clinton
Giving	Bill Clinton
As A Man Thinketh	James Allen
SHIFT – How to reinvent your business, your career, and your personal brand	Peter Arnell
The Spirit of LEADERSHIP, Liberating the Leader in Each of Us	Harrison Owen
Think and Grow Rich – A Black Choice	Dennis Kimbro & Napoleon Hill
Hannibal Crosses the Alps	John Prevas
A Raisin in the Sun	Lorraine Hansberry
To Kill a Mockingbird	Harper Lee
Uncle Tom's Cabin	Harriet Beecher Stowe
Becoming	Michelle Obama

Book Titles	Author(s)
Notes of a Native Son	James Baldwin
If Beale Street Could Talk	James Baldwin
Giovanni's Room	James Baldwin
Blues for Mister Charlie	James Baldwin
Another Country	James Baldwin
Nobody Knows My Name	James Baldwin
Native Son	Richard Wright
Black Boy	Richard Wiright
Black Gangster	Donald Goines
Dopefiend	Donald Goines
White Mans Justice Black Mans Grief	Donald Goines
Street Players	Donald Goines
Black Girl Lost	Donald Goines
Crime Partners	Donald Goines
Manchild in the Promised Land	Claude Brown
A Raisin in the Sun	Lorraine Hansberry
To Kill a Mockingbird	Harper Lee
Uncle Tom's Cabin	Harriet Beecher Stowe
Hamlet	William Shakespeare
Macbeth	William Shakespeare
Othello	William Shakespeare
Romeo and Juliet	William Shakespeare
Of Mice and Men	John Steinbeck
The Grapes of Wrath	John Steinbeck
The Pearl	John Steinbeck
Cat on a Hot tin Roof	Tennessee Williams
The Glass Menagerie	Tennessee Williams
A Streetcar Named Desire	Tennessee Williams
Little Women	Louise May Alcott
The Miracle Worker	William Gibson

Friends

I have been fortunate my entire life to have great friends who are brothers to me. I have built some great relationships and maintained them for the most part. Some of my friends are more like brothers to me, and we would do just about anything for each other. I have had friends that I have participated in sports with, others I went to school with, some that we lived together, and others where we conducted criminal activity. In my personal opinion, there is really no difference in the relationships. In each case, we were expected to watch each other's back and try to better our lives. None of us came from families of wealth, so we all fully understood that we would have to make our own brakes in life.

My older friends (brothers) included people like True, Civ, Ed, Rad, El Sun, Rem, and some others were great teachers with respect to how they monitored how I moved in the street. They would be bitterly honest with me and not care how it affected me. This was important to me because this made me understand at a young age that life was unfair, and you have to be ready to deal with it.

While the older hustlers allowed me to spend time with them, they always made it clear to me that there would be times that I would be asked to leave if the conversation was over my head. I can remember being privy to conversations with Scottie, who was the "man," scolding Ronnie G on how he operated his business. When Ronnie G wanted to buy the same car as Scottie, he let him know that we were not equals, and you need to wait your turn to buy a car, like me. Scottie pointed out to Ronnie that you know people, but I have friends in the right places. I still remember that conversation as a teenager because it made so much sense. You see, many of you know people, but you don't have friends in the right places. When you start to go out in the streets, you must be able to differentiate between friends and people you know.

My peer friends include Curt, Mike, Anthony C., Atiba, Nick, and Muhammad, who have shared so much with me. We share many things in common, including being married, children, owning homes, a passion for clothing, sports, and having been raised in New York City. All of these men were raised by quality parents and were not as heavily involved in streets. Don't get me wrong. They are no squares and have a few stories. Each one of them I consider my brothers and would do anything for them. In each case, having them as friends stopped me from crossing that line.

Another one of my closet friends hasn't fared so well and has spent a great deal of time behind bars. He is a misunderstood individual whose ability to bring people together has made him very unpopular with the powers that be. Sometimes, he is his own worst enemy, but he also has a huge heart and the ability to do so much more with his life. We also share a lot in common, and I am one of the few people he really trusts. Hopefully, he will get a chance to prove many wrong if he gets another chance. I am riding with you, Homie! Gary C., Billy, Ben, Rick, Junie, Fox (Shaun), Calvin (Micey), Sha (Richard), and Charlie are all my younger brothers, and we spent both street time and quality time over the years. Each one of them can tell you things about me that nobody else knows and vice versa. In most cases, we are all making it, but life changes quickly. If one of us experiences hard times, it affects us all. When a negative cloud is cast upon a group, it brings a negative karma that affects all involved. When I look at other races and their ability to have large groups of people succeed, much of that is based on positive karma. In our communities, we need positive karma so that we can begin to make positive changes in how we live. When you have a group of friends and everyone can come together, and they are taking care of their families, homes, jobs, and financial obligations, it is much easier for them to elevate to a higher ground both individually and as a group. If one person needs help, the others are quick to assist because they know that this individual is going through a tough period. But when the same individual is always having problems and is not taking care of their responsibilities, ultimately, he makes the group weak and affects the overall karma of everyone involved. Don't be the weak link. Don't be the one that everyone accepts less from. If you are this person already, then it is time you changed immediately. If you can't change, then one day, you may find yourself all alone. Eventually, everyone grows tired of the slacker.

The last group I will mention includes Lil, BJ, Sean, and Rich. They are my little brothers, and they are a group that I have shared much with, but they also have their own group relationship like I have with others. There is a significant age differential, and there have been times when they needed to bond like True, Civ, Ed, and I without the older brother around. Each one of them has his own style, and I have a lot of respect for how they live their lives. There have been times when having them in my life kept me young and focused. The commonsense level among the group is extremely high, and the decision making is on par with that. They are a special group that I can call on at any time and believe I have. I can remember at times involving them in criminal activity at a young age, but also doing my best to explain the "game" to them. In each case, they learned quickly, and today we can look back and feel a sense of vindication. Again, good people get involved in the streets, especially in poorer communities, where the desire to have more is escalated due to your surroundings.

I strongly believe that the term "friend" has been abused too often in society. A friend is someone that will go to the grave for you but will also talk you out of ruining your life and theirs. Sometimes, when you say you're riding, it should be to ride home. Some of you are confused about friendship and often make poor decisions on choosing friends and on how to navigate those relationships. As you get older, you will have fewer friends, and that is the way it should be. Life has a way of making that happen. People get caught up in their own lives, which can mean struggle or good fortune. In each case, they move on. How many times have you exchanged numbers with someone you have not seen in a long time, and you have never called them and vice versa? I have made a pledge to myself not to take numbers of people I know I will not call. I don't want to be disrespectful, but

I need to be honest with them. In fairness, please do the same to me if warranted. I will not be offended.

I wish everyone much success and don't have a jealous or envious bone in my body. Due to the many projects I am involved in, I know a lot of people, and for the most part, that is good. I do not confuse those relationships with my friendships, which are precious to me. To be quite honest, I know who my friends are. Do you?

Letter to Homie

What's up, brother:

I hope all is well on your end. As I write this letter, I am really concerned with many of the things that are going on in the hood, especially with our young people. Over the last couple of years, we have seen an increase in deaths contributed to gun violence and so-called gang activity. Many of the young men are very confused, and when disagreements occur, they are quick to use guns to attempt to settle these issues. As you may have heard the other day, a fourteen-year-old girl was killed while traveling on the bus on Sutphin Boulevard. This young lady was not the intended target but an innocent bystander. Her death is another horrible reminder of how much the streets have gotten worse. Many will say that statistics show that murder has decreased over the years, but I question the validity of those numbers. All I can tell you is that I have gone to more funerals for teenagers and have counseled more young people recently than I have ever before.

In our day, many of the people who were involved in street activity owned guns, but it was rare that they actually were used. Nowadays, owning a gun is commonplace, with many even taking them to school. Bullying is another issue that many children are faced with daily. I know, as you read this, you are also confused by the negative behavior. First of all, years ago, there were hustlers, stick-up kids, thieves, low lives, and then the civilians. Some straddled the fence, but most knew their place. Many of the young people today do not know the distinction and end up in situations that they are not prepared to deal with. Some are carrying pistols with no intention of using them, which makes them even more dangerous. Others are the victims of peer pressure and may pull the trigger rather than feel a sense of embarrassment from their so-called friends. We also have those who have already determined that having a reputation as a "killer" is a status that they can be proud of as opposed to graduating college or taking on a successful career.

As I view everything around our young people, I am not one to blame the music or the lifestyle. I am not one to blame the cellphones, videos, Twitter, Facebook, Instagram, or R-rated movies. I strongly believe that we have done a horrible job in the Black community, especially the men, in dealing with young Black boys. In our day, men in the street, at times, would look to discourage boys from emulating their lifestyles. Yes, there were some that they would take under their wing, but never the majority. Today, there is no sense of community. Everyone gets a package. We need to be honest with our young people about the pitfalls that await them.

You, like me, were part of the streets at a young age and have seen an experienced a lot of different things in your life. Many of the young people in the streets have tunnel vision and have their focus on cars, clothes, jewelry and getting high, a lifestyle that we both know cannot be sustained for a long period of time. They do not trust the establishment, which may include Black doctors, lawyers, clergy, politicians, educators, and others, because they believe their views are condescending, and reaching their level in life is not attainable. They look at the rappers, professional athletes, and the streets as their only road to success. Social media has only elevated this passion for this rich and famous lifestyle.

You are still someone who has a voice and has actually lived the life that they think they want. You are still revered in many circles, and your mind is sharp as ever. You have survived so much, and I strongly believe you can offer a pathway for some of these confused young people in the streets. They need to hear from somebody they can identify with because, like you, many of them have intelligence and talent that they can put to good use before it is too late. The American prison system is full of young Black men and women who never had a chance. Let's give them one now.

Can you please provide some direction for our youths? Others have failed horribly, and it's not their fault they can't connect to the streets. We will never be able to change the poor conditions of our communities until we can better the lives in the streets. In the end, the streets matter more than anything else.

Your cooperation is appreciated and needed.

Your Brother,

G

Cancer

In August of 2018, approaching my fifty-eighth birthday, I was diagnosed with prostate cancer, and it was a huge shock to me. I have always done a great job of taking care of myself, including working out consistently (at least five days a week), eating pretty well, and getting routine check-ups. My earlier check-ups had revealed a high prostate-specific antigen (PSA) count, which is the measurement for the potential of prostate cancer. My doctors continued to check this over approximately a year, but my count continued to rise. Eventually, I was scheduled for a biopsy, which is a medical test commonly performed by a surgeon, interventional radiologist, or an interventional cardiologist involving the extraction of sample cells or tissues for examination to determine the presence or extent of a disease. The tissue is generally examined under a microscope by a pathologist and can also be analyzed chemically. My biopsy revealed cancer, and to my wife and me, it was a shock. Never in my life would I expect to have cancer. There were no major signs except more frequent urination, but that could be contributed to many things, including my age. After pulling myself together, my next step was to tell my three daughters. The irony was on this particular day, they happened to be all together, and my wife and I went there to reveal the horrible news. Once settling in, I asked them to come into a vacant room so that we did not alarm the children. After hesitating, I dropped the news, and as expected, they all lost it, and I went from being the wounded to the protector and knew at that moment, I had to pull myself together. My wife did a great job of being the rock that day and many others throughout the entire process. After the tears had cleared, we assured them with the proper care that was a great chance I could be cured. Sitting there that day, I came to the realization that I had to turn my ordeal to a positive situation, so we began to plan an event to bring exposure to prostate cancer and how we could increase prostate and other forms of cancer awareness. Our goal was to get people to get tested, assist those dealing with cancer and work with families that had a family member dealing with cancer. We started putting it together immediately, and it gave us a

195

temporary relief of all the pain we each were going through. Imagine that we were all shell shocked, but we jumped into fight mode because that is the DNA of our family. My wife and I displayed leadership, and my children took it from there, and they ran with it. They were not going to be a pity party. We were going to turn a negative to a positive, and that is what we did. The event was held on September 23rd, 2018, my fifty-eighth birthday, and was a huge success. We held the event at our restaurant, and people came from all over, and those who couldn't come donated to the cause. I was so proud of my family that day and through the entire process. After this event, we held several other events dedicated to cancer, and we have pledged to continue these events through R.I.S.E., my non-profit organization, each year.

Cancer was tough for me mentally. People are quick to say you will be all right or don't worry, but that is bullshit. You are scared because things can change quickly, and you can go from maintaining to your deathbed with no notice. Just as there are people who recover, there are people who die. I was scared for myself, but I was more scared for my family. Part of me felt as if I was letting them down. I have never been that vulnerable in my life. My only other time of ever being hospitalized was when I tore my Achilles tendon, and that was nothing compared to cancer.

My research below, that I will share with you so you can be more familiar with prostate cancer, includes the following:

Black men are still more likely to get prostate cancer and to die from it than white men, and this is one of the most dramatic disparities in cancer.

There are numerous racial differences in the expression of genes involved with cancer development. Also, Black men are more likely to be obese, and obesity is related to increased incidence and mortality related to prostate cancer as well as potential genetic links between obesity and prostate cancer.

The potential environmental factors may be related to both personal behavior and a greater likelihood to live/work in unfriendly ecological settings. It is possible that a greater tendency to eat a diet that contains more meat, high fat, fewer plant-based antioxidants, and more processed foods with greater amounts of chemical preservatives may increase the risk for prostate cancer development. In addition, Black men are more likely to live in areas that have greater proximity to environmental toxins from industrial waste, sewage processing plants, and areas with poorer air quality. Black men may have more exposure to occupational chemicals related to pesticides, organic solvents used for cleaning, and industrial fumes in multiple manufacturing and processing plants.

Recent studies suggest that black men might benefit from screening for prostate cancer ten years earlier than the current national screening guideline recommends (age 55). Such screening involves testing a man's blood for levels of a marker called PSA, which can indicate the presence of cancer. However, screening comes with risks—most notably, the risk of treating cancer that may be too slow-growing to cause the man harm. So, the risks and benefits of screening must be carefully balanced.

Statistically, Black men have nearly a 50% higher incidence of prostate cancer when compared to white men, and twice the mortality. We also know that Black men develop prostate cancer at an earlier age with higher PSA levels than white men and that they tend to develop a more aggressive disease based on the Gleason scores. Black men also tend to have more advanced disease at the time of diagnosis when compared to white men. According to one major study, this risk for advanced disease persists even after adjusting for socioeconomic, clinical, and pathologic variables. The exact reason for the disparity in the incidence of prostate cancer in Black men is not completely clear but is thought to be a combination of dietary and genetic factors. The even greater disparity in prostate cancer mortality in these men is probably due, in large part, to lack of routine screening,

197

poor access to health care, and more advanced disease at the time of diagnosis, which certainly impacts the treatment outcomes.

My family went through the entire process with me, as did close friends and the community itself. I made a decision that I would join social media (Facebook & Instagram), where I shared my battle with cancer. Previously I had no desire to be a part of social media because I felt many people went overboard, and I didn't want to associate myself with that lifestyle. After much thought and consulting people I trusted, I came to the conclusion if I used social media in a positive way, I could help so many others through sharing my story. It was important to me to do my part, encouraging others to get tested, so they did not have to endure what I was going through. So far, I think it has been successful, and I will continue to share my story. My social media presence is a combination of my personal and community work and the programs we offer through R.I.S.E., which we look to make more visible. I should have probably done this sooner. So, in a strange way, cancer has motivated me and increased our efforts to assist other people.

As I write this, I am awaiting my six-month evaluation to determine if I am cancer-free, which I have done for a year now. Every six months, I have to have this testing to ensure I am still cancer-free. I am a little nervous, but I trust the process better at this point. In the beginning, I was working with some doctors who clearly did not have my best interest in mind, which is the case for many people. They refer you to their colleagues, with all of them trying to maximize the profit by sending you back and forth to each other taking unneeded tests while you are suffering both physically and mentally. I was fortunate that I had a family member in the medical field who rescued me by finding me the right doctors who treated me well. I will always be thankful to Debbie; she is an angel to me. I was confused, and my wife advised me to speak with Debbie, and she took over from there. She scheduled my appointments with doctors that I normally would not have been able to see that quickly. She followed up with me. She showed up to my appointments. She was there through my surgery, and when I was discharged, she was there with a take-home kit with everything I would need for my recovery. When I was home alone recovering, I thought of Debbie and what she had done for me, and for about ten minutes, I cried. I mean, I really cried because I could not believe that someone would go out of their way like she did. Not everyone will have a Debbie in their life. That is why it is important that men take care of themselves better. Cancer destroys lives. Families sometimes never recover when a family member contracts cancer.

During this period of dealing with Cancer, many people reached out to me on a regular basis. One person in particular was Dave Edwards Jr. Dave and I have a relationship that goes back to his childhood, and we were very close. He would always reach out to me to check on me and seek advice on multiple issues. If you know Dave, then you know he exemplifies the spirit of New York City folklore, an educated basketball legend with a street pedigree and most of all a high degree of common sense with the gift of gab to go with it. Dave would call me every week and in his own way pull me up. "G you alright? You know I need you to get this shit together. I need you to get better. You need anything? Alright, you know I love you." Recently Dave died due to COVID-19, and it was a shock to many people. When I got the news, it broke my heart. When I think about him and Jermaine Miller, each day I have to catch myself. Dave was special having been a high school legend that played at both Georgetown (under John Thompson) and Texas AM. Dave is a product of the lengendary Edwards family of South Jamaica. Dave was doing some amazing work with children for many years before this and will be missed by many. I love you baby bro

I will dedicate part of my life to assisting others with cancer. I think it is the least I can do after being affected. I pray for those who are dealing with cancer each day. Thank you to all of my supporters. I will never forget you.

Final Thoughts

Many will read my book and immediately be offended by some of the things I have expressed. Some will take issue with my use of the word "nigga" and why I chose to use it. I recently read an article in *Ebony* magazine, where Samuel Jackson expressed his views on the word "nigga" and why he continues to use it. Part of the interview contains the following:

> Nigga became a part of my vocabulary when I was born. How so? Because it was used on me in my house often. "Nigga, you crazy." My mom, my grandmom, my granddad, my relatives, my neighbors. I know the word nigga as an admonishment, an endearment, a criticism, and an invective. So, I use it; I don't run from it. I don't have an issue with it or who says it. I always put it the context of how it was used on me.

After I read this piece, I went back and read what I had written on the subject and thought my views consistent with his. I do not know Samuel Jackson but have always enjoyed his interviews and the things he has expressed. Like Jay-Z, they are strong Black men who stick to their guns and didn't waver on their use of the word. In Jay-Z's book, *Decoded*, he offers this quote:

> Oprah, for instance, still can't get past the n-word issue (or the nigga issue, with all apologies to Ms. Winfrey). I can respect her position. To her, it's a matter of acknowledging the deep and painful history of the word. To me, it's just a word, a word whose power is owned by the user and his or her intention. People give words power, so banning a word is futile, really. "Nigga" becomes "porch monkey," becomes "coon" and so on if that's what is in a person's heart. The key is to change the person. We change people through conversation, not through censorship.

Again, I will continue to use the word, but I hope others will understand, so we can all focus on more pressing issues concerning our communities. Remember, actions speak louder than words.

One of the primary reasons I wrote this book was to reveal who I was to my grandchildren. I never had a relationship with my father, grandparents on either side, or most of my family. I wanted my legacy to be available to them so they would have a reference to exactly who Poppa is. I am not ashamed of anything I have chosen to reveal and, in fact, very proud of the man I have become. My aunt, who I believe watches over me, told me at a young age that your good must outweigh your bad, and if you do that, you are on the right track. I strongly believe my good far outweighs my bad, and if there is a Heaven, I won't have to wait in line. Someone once asked me to define myself in one sentence, and I replied, "I am a very good person that has done some bad things." That definition probably defines some of the people I grew up with as well.

My life has been just that—my life. While I have done things that some would consider wrong, I have done many things that they would consider honorable. I have always been part of the New York City streets, sometimes directly, other times, with my association with others, and with the programs, I have operated. I have spent my entire life around young people, and, in many ways, it has kept me fit and alert. I strongly believe, for a Black man, I am as well rounded as anyone that I have ever met. I fully understand that sometimes old can be better than new, that good people do bad things, and that love can be blind. I still have hope for Black America, but I am also very realistic about our chances. We must decrease the teenage pregnancy percentage, start to plan a family, prioritize safe sex, and familiarize our children with modern diversified family structures. Men, where required, must become a consistent figure in the lives of their children no matter how many children they have. I grew up without a father, so I fully understand the importance of male leadership. Once I became a father, it became and is still, to this day, my top priority with being a grandfather equal to it. These parental roles must be valued and treasured.

I wonder, will the streets return to a time when there can be a fair fight, and if you lose, you can accept it and move on? I wonder if common sense will prevail, and whether we will have corporate executives continue to take bonuses while employees of their companies are laid off. I wonder if organizations like the NCAA will continue to make billions off of the backs of children, particularly Black ones, while hiding under the banner of amateur athletics. I wonder if the Black community will ever decide to work together to improve the overall conditions we live under for the sake of our children. I wonder if true education exists in any school, either public or private. I wonder if some educators have the goal of uplifting communities and not molesting the children they teach. I fully understand that your drug of choice or addiction will decide your life and that there are functional addicts who perform better than non-users.

In my sixty years, I have seen, heard, and experienced a lot. I have met some people with a gun in their waistbands who I would trust before some corporate types and educators I have worked with. Occupations do not define character. We all have witnessed law enforcement, clergy, politicians, doctors, and other professions that have done horrible things in life. If you are a piece of shit, then you are a piece of shit. Sometimes, we look the other way. Other times, you just have a short memory, but you know the facts. Many of us carry around emotional scars forever. However, as sad as it may seem, you must try your best to get over it. Relatives, parents, husbands, wives, lovers, co-workers, all at times, make bad decisions that can affect others. You have to make a decision on what you can live with, and then begin to either repair the damage or move on. Life is short, and you cannot afford to allow time to pass in limbo.

Character is what separates people. No matter how you earn at the end of the day, how you treat people will define your existence. I have been an advocate for children my entire life. I believe children have been getting a raw deal from adults forever. They do not ask to come into this world, and once they get here, many adults are not prepared to take care of them. Many are abused and suffer throughout their lives.

Moving forward, I hope people who read this book will begin to understand the importance of being a great parent. I have had the honor of raising my children, along with my wife, in a system that worked for us as a family. In some ways, it was very traditional; in others, it was very different. My wife and I, at times, sit back and reflect on the experiences as parents and have no regrets. We are proud of the job we have done and the three beautiful daughters we have raised. However, we also are practicing every day to be great grandparents, a role we also will take great pride in. Being a good grandparent sometimes means being a tougher parent. To clarify, there will be times when you need to check your kids on their lives because now it affects your grandchildren. They will take offense, a natural reaction, but who cares? If your intentions are good, so be it. Building a family legacy of success requires strong leadership. Being a strong leader requires you to say things that need to be said. Remember the children at the end of the day.

There will be times when money and your financial well-being will be your priority, and others when building the family legacy is more important. Sometimes, you have encountered financial struggles to build character. Remember that. Believe in yourself. You will always find a way to earn, but once you sell your soul to the devil, it is almost impossible to get back. Have a line that you do not cross. That strategy has always worked for me.

Bad news will be a part of your life, and how you handle it will say even more about you. My mother's favorite saying is, "It's not what happens to you. It's what you do when it happens." This saying applies to everyone, so take heed and be ready.

I can say with great conviction that when I rise each day, I have every intention of doing the right thing. However, I am honest enough to admit there may be times when what society has established as right is not always right for the people, especially the children I represent. Some of the rules make no sense from a commonsense perspective, so I ask myself: Do I follow rules that make no sense or do what makes sense and help those in need? I have written this book for the many street soldiers who will identify with my experiences. They will see some similarities and gravitate to the positive messages in each chapter. I hope that they find my passion for fatherhood and establish programs in their communities to assist people in need. I hope that they think twice about leaving their homes with their guns and attempt to squash beefs before someone is murdered. I hope that they never put their hands on women and know when to get out of the drug game before it is too late. I hope that some people who are not Black and Hispanic will start to understand that just because we have spent time in jail and the streets that we can perform at a high level if given a chance.

I have chosen Dr. Bernard Gassaway to do the "Introduction" to my book. Gass, as I commonly refer to him, is someone who knows me very well, and he is someone that I trust dearly. Over the years, we have impacted the lives of many youths and adults as a team and individuals. He has walked me through this entire process, and it would not have been possible without his mentorship. For those of you that are not familiar with him, please do your research because he is one of the *most prized* educators and advocates for children in the country.

I have also chosen my childhood friend, Kenneth Supreme McGriff, to do the closing to my book. While this may raise some eyebrows, that is fine. My intentions are to reach the many young people in the streets that have gone astray. Preme is someone that still has an enormous amount of popularity, whether you like it or not. One of my goals is to be realistic regarding the voices that people in the streets will respect and take seriously, and he fills that void. Again, let me emphasize the groups that have the necessary appeal in the hood include NBA/NFL players, rap music and R&B music affiliated people, TV/movie personalities, and people from the streets. No others need to apply. If you are trying to reach the streets, you have to speak the language, and these groups speak it fluently.

My last point is to draw a comparison to both gentlemen. Gass and Preme are very similar in many ways. Barring some early decisions in life, Gass was a misguided youth who was on his way to a life of crime until his life changed. He eventually turned his life around and went on to become a legendary educator earning his doctorate from Columbia University.

Preme is an exceptional leader who has displayed a variety of skills other than his attachment to the street, including directing the movie "Crime Partners." Preme is firmly established in street folklore, and to some, that is not something to be proud of, but it is our reality. To make it plain and simple, their roles could have been reversed many years ago, depending on what could happen on any given day in the hood. That is the fine line you walk being a Black male in America.

Last, I will never make the New York Times Best Seller List considering some of the things that I have been involved with in my life and have written, but I truly believe I have a place in Heaven even though I have passed through Hell.

Love my Real Niggas! G

Closing

Kenneth Supreme McGriff

Sent from United States Penitentiary McCreary-Pine Knot, Kentucky

To my brother and Friend Gary Clifton, I've sat for days contemplating what words I could convey to aid the young brothers coming up in the hood as we did. Knowing that when we are young, there is little we feel we don't already know. The difference with them and us is when we were young, we sought counsel from our older Homie's and elders. Wise men always seek counsel and advice.

What I believe is a good way to start this dialog (conversation) with them (my young brothers) is to share our bond and friendship. Gary and I grew up around each other and shared all the same friends, but we did our own thing. The friendship we had grew organically. We saw a lot in each other and became closer by choice. Even though our lives took different turns. G took the right path (the long way). While I wouldn't say I took the wrong path, because my ultimate goal was to get out the game and have successful legitimate businesses. But I took the short cut, (funny thing is the short cut is really the long way) filled with obstacles, danger, and death. It's the White Man's trap for us; the short path is where they make all the rules, and you can't win! Once you step on that path, they get to define you, whether its true or not, as they have done me. So every time I was in transition looking for the exit to change my life, starting a new legit business, the devil would appear. We wont let you leave; die a drug dealer as we've defined you. We must learn to exist within the already established rules. Once we learn and master the rules, we can accomplish any of our goals, without interference from the devil. (To break the rules, you must first master them.).

So as G would always say, as you get older, your circle of friends should get smaller and tighter; you learn to weed out the fake one's and discover the real ones. When I became entangled in my current situation, Gary did not distance himself; actually he got deeper involved. He testified at my Death Penalty Trial, and when I got sent to Supermax ADX, to try and break me, Gary was the first person to visit me there (a concrete tomb). And he has been doing this life until death sentence with me, because he knows my heart and knew the plans I had when I started my film company and soundtrack business. I got to finish my dream of making a "Donald Goines" novel into a film and soundtrack (Crime Partners, 2003).

When I found out that my brother Gary had cancer (another form of death sentence), I kept reminding him of the cloth we were cut from, that he would beat it, that he had to beat it, that he had to beat it because people depended on his presence and wisdom, myself included. So for the youngsters reading this, that's what real friendship is. It lasts forever, and you should value it. But you must respect each other. So if any of you younger guys out there get a chance, listen to my man "G"; he's a Real Nigga, and he will guide you to govern yourself accordingly.

Friends don't kill friends. Conflict resolution is a must; have weapon in the arsenal of real soldiers. When we were growing up, it was always about respect. You must give respect to get respect. We had guns, but they were rarely if ever used, because murder is forever. The only time a gun should be used is in self-defense, to defend only. Only a dumb nigga wants a body! George Jackson always said, "Settle your petty quarrels and come together." The worst label you can have is a killer; you are then limited, and it is only a matter of time. A killer is never more important than an earner (businessman); no one wants to be around a killer, because a killer can't be trusted implicitly.

I am writing this letter almost 20 years into 8 life sentences because my brother Gary asked me to. He was concerned enough with the behavior of some of your youngsters who don't understand consequence. If you want to avoid hazards, you must understand consequence. The wise man seeks peace; be wise. Gary felt because of all the struggles and fights and suffering I've endured, fighting some of the most powerful people in the world, and still I stand tall, and continue to fight. Maybe I could share some insight that could be useful to some of the young brothers, and might even save a few. Malcolm X said, "That if you want to learn, study those that have the power (the White man). Learn their chess moves and stop playing checkers." They sit in smoke filled rooms and plan and plot how to keep us down. They are strategic! The biggest stragem (trick) is the NRA, these devils figured it all out, flood the cities with guns, easier to buy than cigarettes. They get rich from all of our money, and then we slaughter each other with their weapons over petty beefs. They get our money, kills us off, and put the killers under the jail. So what stragem do you'll have? If left to our own devices we will destroy ourselves. They continue to apply the same old Willie Lynch tactics, to make us hate ourselves. The real enemy and our greatest challenge in the Black community is the abundance of guns, and the gun manufacturers and the gun industry (NRA), they are the real problem.

One of the most misguided statements I ever heard was "defund the police"; what does that mean? I've been in the streets most of my life, and even I know you must have order; without rules, there is chaos. But I agree the police must respect the law as well, and respect the right of all citizens they are sworn to protect. But you can't use incendiary slogans in a fit of emotions; it only confuses people and hurts your cause. Then the opposition uses it as a weapon against you. Messaging is critical to outcome; you must think before you speak!

I know the culture and mentality of the police; they have a gangster mentality and they stick together, no matter how wrong. They look at every one as a perp (perpetrator), them against us. That's where the problem starts. When I was 15, hanging in the Rochdale Mall, the Police detained us and I'll never forget his words; he said, "You think your tough, well you're not, we're tough, we're the biggest, baddest, gang there is"; I never forgot those words, and it's true, and they know it. When fighting a war you must have a plan to be genuinely empowered when fighting an invincible beast; you must kill it from within; you must wage resistance from inside the system and defeat it with its own rules. Fighting for your rights is liberating and as long as you're fighting, you are free, so never stop fighting. But stop fighting and killing each other! The real enemy is racism and oppression and the subtle way in which they implement it. They deal with us with hate, but not with others. They never describe the shooter of the Mother Emanuel Church or the shooter of Marjory Stoneman Douglas High School, like they describe us. They deal with them without hate with care and understanding, why?

Hopefully my words reach some of you. I've given you some insight beforehand of what your life can become. If you're smart you will not encounter my missteps. I wish you all well. Remember the violent man measures his worth by the distorted criterion of his physical impact rather than his ability to pursue a life plan (Goal). Violent men are basically children who have learned to use force to resolve everything no matter how small or petty. Think about it first always!

Farewell brother Gary, keep fighting for our youth, I will aid in any capacity necessary.

Kenneth Supreme McGriff

About the Author

Gary B. Clifton is a product of Jamaica, Queens, New York, where he was educated in the New York City Public School System. After attending several colleges to learn political science, business administration, and management, he entered corporate America, where he worked for twenty-five years as a senior corporate manager. During his time in corporate America, he was responsible for initiating many successful programs, including a diversity program, Black Male Employment Initiative, and several programs designed to increase awareness of the inequality of people of color in corporate America. During this time, Gary also returned to the classroom, where he embraced new ways of learning and enhanced his managerial skills. Gary retired from corporate America in 2004 to pursue his entrepreneurial calling and open several successful businesses.

Gary started Recreational Inner-City Sports & Education (R.I.S.E.) in 1982. R.I.S.E. is a non-profit educational and recreational organization that has serviced thousands of youth over the last thirty-five years. R.I.S.E. has always remained true to its roots as a very resourceful and trusted grassroots organization with great influence in the Black community. Our mission includes:

- Combat drug abuse, gang violence, and proliferation
- Collaborate with various organizations to increase program options for youths
- Develop programs to meet the needs of a diverse adolescent community
- Mentor children, fathers, families, and prospective educators
- Offer educational seminars for youths, parents, and educators
- Utilize sports and recreation to educate, motivate, and create trust

R.I.S.E. operates primarily from MS 72 in Rochdale Village (Jamaica) but provides programs throughout New York City.

R.I.S.E. also maintains a satellite office in the financial district in downtown New York City for administrative purposes. R.I.S.E. receives support from both private and public donors. The majority of R.I.S.E. participants have gone on to lead positive lives, including some as professional athletes, educators, attorneys, doctors, and corporate leaders. R.I.S.E. also plays a valuable role on the New York City streets serving as a liaison for conflicts, disputes, and creating opportunities for people in need of direction.

Gary is married to his wife of thirty-eight years, Toni. Gary, Toni, and family have owned and operated several successful businesses over the years, including Pretty Toni's Café. Pretty Toni's Café is a successful soul food restaurant that opened in 2009. Gary and Toni have three daughters Temiko, Tonita, and Toi, who are all college graduates and, in addition to their own careers, assist in managing the family businesses. The Cliftons have seven grandchildren who they take great pride in.

Gary is proud of the example he has set as a Black man in America. Coming from a single-parent home in a very tough community was always challenging. He credits his family with keeping him focused and believes that the community he came from is worth fighting for. The Cliftons currently reside in Valley Stream, New York but will always consider Jamaica, Queens, their home in Queens.

Made in the USA
Middletown, DE
10 April 2023

28510903R00124